sept. 2017

WHERE ON EARTH?

Written by James Doyle
Illustrated by Andrew Pinder
Edited by Sue McMillan, Elizabeth Scoggins,
Nicola Baxter and Sally Pilkington

Designed by Zoe Bradley
Cover Illustrated by Hui Skipp
Cover Designed by Angie Allison
and Amy Cooper

For Oonágh, Conall, Erin and Cara

WHERE ON EARTH

Buster Books

This paperback edition first published in 2017

First published in Great Britain in 2010 by Buster Books,
an imprint of Michael O'Mara Books Limited,
9 Lion Yard, Tremadoc Road, London SW4 7NQ

W www.busterbooks.co.uk f Buster Children's Books @BusterBooks

Every reasonable effort has been made to acknowledge all copyright holders. Any errors
or omissions that may have occurred are inadvertent, and anyone with any copyright
queries is invited to write to the publishers, so that a full acknowledgement may be
included in subsequent editions of this work.

A CIP catalogue record for this book is available from the British Library.

ISBN: 978–1–78055–468–6

1 3 5 7 9 10 8 6 4 2

Printed and bound in March 2017 by CPI Group (UK) Ltd,
108 Beddington Lane, Croydon, CR0 4YY, United Kingdom.

Papers used by Michael O'Mara Books are natural, recyclable products
made from wood grown in sustainable forests. The manufacturing processes
conform to the environmental regulations of the country of origin.

CONTENTS

WELCOME TO THE WORLD

Have you ever pondered who would win in a fight between a polar bear and a penguin, or wondered why everyone goes on about how important rainforests are?

Have you ever asked yourself, 'How do hurricanes happen?' and, 'What makes a mountain?'

All these questions and many more are answered in this brilliant book. It's packed with information about the amazing planet we live on. There are sections on its record-breaking physical features, from mountains and deserts to islands and oceans. Read about its worst natural hazards, from earthquakes and volcanic eruptions to wildfires and whirlwinds. Don't miss the section that makes sense of maps. Filled with fascinating facts and statistics, this book even has a continent-by-continent list of countries and their capitals.

Soon you will be able to answer anyone who asks 'What is the difference between an ocean and a sea?' or 'Where on Earth is the tallest waterfall?'

The world is at your fingertips.

THE EARTH

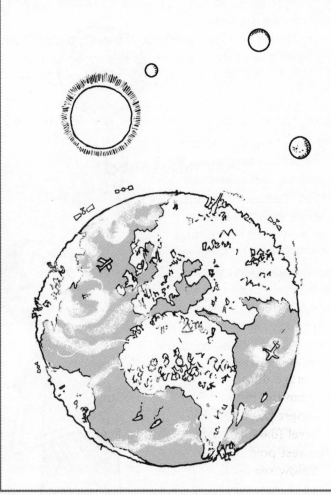

HOME, SWEET HOME!

Earth, the planet you call home, is one of a group of eight planets that move around the Sun. These planets in order of closeness to the Sun are: Mercury, Venus, Earth, Mars, Jupiter, Saturn, Uranus and Neptune. Together, they make up what is known as the solar system.

Until recently, Pluto was considered the ninth planet in the solar system. It is smaller than the Earth's moon and, in 2006, scientists decided to reclassify it as a 'dwarf planet'.

Planet Earth is very special. No other planet in the solar system has been found to support life – and at present it is the only one known to do so in the whole universe.

Earth's Vital Statistics

Age	4.5 – 4.6 billion years
Distance around the equator (the middle)	40,075 kilometres (or km)
Surface area	510,065,700 square kilometres (or km²)
Mass	6,000 billion billion tonnes
Area covered by land	148,940,000km²
Area covered by sea	361,132,000km²
Average distance from the Sun	150,000,000km
Average distance from the Moon	384,000km
Highest point above sea level (8,848 metres)	Mount Everest, Nepal
Lowest point on land below sea level (417 metres)	The Dead Sea, Israel/Jordan

It's A Small World After All

The Earth sometimes feels like a huge place, but in fact, it is only the fifth largest planet in the Solar System. Jupiter is the biggest – its diameter is 11 times that of Earth.

What Is The World Made Of?

Earth is known as a 'terrestrial' planet, which means it is mostly made from rock, rather than gas. It is made up of three main layers.

The crust. This is the outer layer of the Earth. It is about 8 km thick under the oceans, and up to 40 km thick under the continents. It is mostly made of granite and basalt – two types of rock made by volcanoes. Human beings live on this solid outer surface.

The mantle. Under the crust is the mantle. The mantle is about 2,900 km thick. With temperatures reaching nearly 2,000°C, the mantle rock is so hot that it has partly melted into thick, gooey, molten rock, called magma.

The core. The Earth's core is so deep below the surface that scientists aren't entirely sure what it is made of. They believe it is made mostly of iron and nickel, and that it is extremely hot, with temperatures of over 7,000°C! The outer core is about 2,250 km thick and is liquid. The inner core is about 2,600 km in diameter. Despite the scorching temperatures, the inner core is thought to be solid, due to the weight of the layers above pressing down on it.

Journey To The Centre Of The Earth

The distance from the Earth's surface to the centre is about 6,400km. However, you could never actually make a journey to the centre of the Earth – you'd either be fried to a crisp in the scorching heat, or crushed to death by the huge pressure of the layers above.

Crust

Mantle

Outer core

Inner core

Cracks In The Crust

The Earth's crust is broken into pieces, like a giant jigsaw puzzle. These pieces are called plates. There are seven enormous plates, and many smaller ones. The study of how the plates move is called plate tectonics. The plates float on the partially melted mantle, which moves them slowly over the Earth's surface. Most of the plate edges, or boundaries, are under the sea and move only a few centimetres a year.

The Enormous Plates

African Plate
Antarctic Plate
Eurasian Plate
Indo-Australian Plate
North American Plate
Pacific Plate
South American Plate

The Biggest Small Plates

Arabian Plate
Caribbean Plate
Cocos Plate
Juan de Fuca Plate
Nazca Plate
Philippine Plate
Scotia Plate

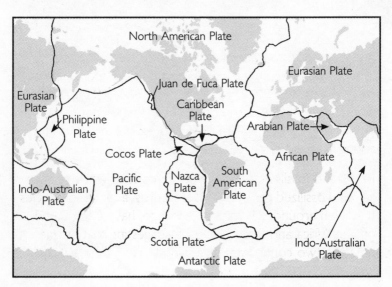

Drifting Apart

Did you know that all the land on Earth was at one time joined together in one great continent, called Pangaea? The first person to suggest this was a German geographer named Alfred Wegener (1880–1930).

Wegener noticed that on a map the shape of the east coast of South America looked as if it fitted into the west coast of Africa. When he watched icebergs drifting out to sea in Greenland, he realized that the continents must be moving, too. However, it was not until the 1960s that scientists could prove his theory.

Rocks and fossils also show that the continents were once joined. Fossilized remains of Mesosaurus, a dinosaur species that lived around 300 million years ago, have been found only in Africa and South America, suggesting that at one time the two continents were joined.

Continents On The Move

The world has changed a lot in the last 250 million years. These maps show you how the continents are thought to have moved in this time.

250 Million Years Ago.

The continents formed one enormous land mass, called 'Pangaea' which means 'all lands' in ancient Greek. It was surrounded by a huge ocean, called 'Panthalassa', which means 'all seas'.

200 Million Years Ago.

Pangaea started to split into two giant continents – 'Laurasia' in the north and 'Gondwana' in the south.

135 Million Years Ago. The two giant continents started to split once more. Gondwana divided into Africa and South America, separated by the Atlantic Ocean. India broke off to form a separate island continent and drifted north.

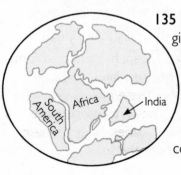

40 Million Years Ago. The continents began to look more like they do today. Australia and Antarctica started drifting apart. India collided with the continent of Eurasia. North America and Greenland shifted west, splitting away from Eurasia. Later, Greenland was left as an island by rising sea levels (see page 68).

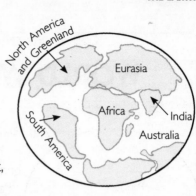

Present Day Planet Earth

The world has not stopped changing as the Earth's tectonic plates are constantly on the move. Some plates are shifting towards each other. As these plates move together, one plate gets pushed under the other, the rock melts and it becomes part of the Earth's mantle. These boundaries are called destructive boundaries because land is destroyed.

However, new land is created all the time. When plates pull away from one another, molten rock, or magma, is released into the gap, hardening to form new land.

These points are known as constructive boundaries. Most of these are under the sea.

WORLD WEATHER

HOW DOES WEATHER WORK?

Weather affects every living thing on Earth and it is always changing – but how does it work, and why does it change?

A Planet With An Atmosphere

The atmosphere is a thin layer of gases covering the planet. It protects Earth from the solar system's extreme temperatures. Earth's closest neighbours, Mars and Venus, are unable to support life, as their atmospheres don't produce the right conditions. Mars, which is further from the Sun, is freezing, and Venus, which is closer, has a thick, insulating atmosphere, making it too hot for life to exist.

Earth's weather is contained in the layer of atmosphere closest to the surface, called the 'troposphere'. It is only 16km thick at the equator, and even thinner at the poles, where it is only 7km high. In fact, it is so thin that if you looked at a model of the Earth (a globe), the troposphere would be thinner than a coat of varnish on the surface!

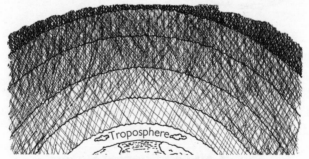

Troposphere

What's The Difference?

'Weather' is the hour-to-hour or day-to-day state of the atmosphere. 'Climate' describes the state of the atmosphere over a much longer period (usually at least 30 years).

The Hot And Cold Of It

Planet Earth is a spinning ball of rock. It takes 24 hours – a day – for the Earth to complete one spin. As it spins, the Earth is also moving in a path, or 'orbit', around the Sun. Radiation from the Sun heats the planet, but it is not warmed evenly. A band around the middle of the planet, called the 'tropics', receives more heat than the parts at the top and bottom, which are known as the 'poles'.

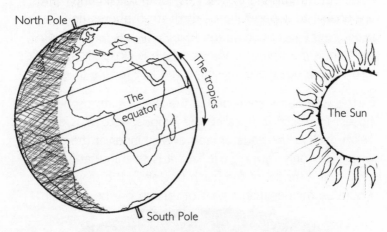

The difference in temperatures explains why there are warm, tropical rainforests and hot, dry deserts near the equator and frozen wastelands at the North and South Poles. Temperatures would be even more extreme in these areas if there weren't some very clever things going on in the atmosphere.

Earth's Air-Conditioning System

Heat from the Sun is moved from warmer parts of Earth to cooler areas by the constant movement of ocean currents, winds and big storms, such as hurricanes, which redistribute heat more evenly.

Think of this as being the Earth's very own heating and air-conditioning system. Balancing the temperature around the world makes Earth the perfect planet for life. Without these circulation systems, Earth's poles would be much colder and the tropics would be far too hot. Some people even think that life on Earth would not be possible without them.

The Reason For Seasons

If you look at a model of the Earth, you will see that the planet's axis – the imaginary line through the centre around which it rotates – is tilted to one side. Earth travels around the Sun once each year. The path it follows is called the orbit. As it moves, the tilt means that different parts of the planet get more sunshine at different times of the year.

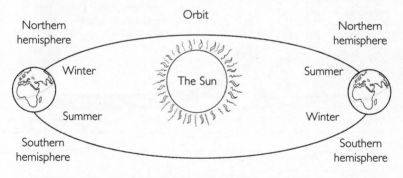

During Earth's orbit the seasons change. When it is winter in the north, the northern hemisphere is tilted away from the Sun. The weather is cooler as it doesn't get much heat and light. Meanwhile, it is summer in the warmer southern hemisphere, as it gets more hours of sunlight each day. As the Earth's orbit continues, the northern hemisphere starts to get more sunlight each day and summer comes. At the same time, it is winter in the southern hemisphere.

Blowing In The Wind

Most air and water movement on Earth is the result of changes in temperature and 'air pressure'. Air pressure is caused by the weight of gases in the atmosphere pushing down on the surface of the Earth. A difference in temperature between places, such as sea and land, creates differences in pressure. Cooler air is denser, so it falls. Warmer air is lighter, so it rises.

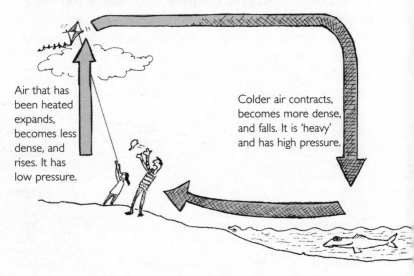

Air that has been heated expands, becomes less dense, and rises. It has low pressure.

Colder air contracts, becomes more dense, and falls. It is 'heavy' and has high pressure.

Winds form as a result of these differences in pressure. A wind is created when air moves from an area of high pressure to an area of low pressure. The greater the difference between the area of high pressure and the area of low pressure, the faster the wind blows.

You can 'make' your own wind quite simply by blowing up a balloon. The air inside the balloon is at higher pressure than the air outside it. Hold the balloon in front of you and let go – *whoosh*! ... your very own wind.

'Water' You Talking About?

Did you know that much of the water around today is the same water that fell thousands of years ago? Water can be splashing around in the ocean one week and by the next week fall on your head as rain. This process is called the 'water cycle' and is shown below. It is continually recycling and cleaning the water on planet Earth.

To fully understand how the water cycle works, you need to know your '-ations':

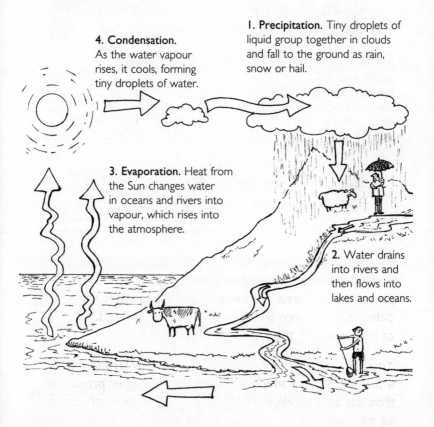

4. Condensation.
As the water vapour rises, it cools, forming tiny droplets of water.

I. Precipitation. Tiny droplets of liquid group together in clouds and fall to the ground as rain, snow or hail.

3. Evaporation. Heat from the Sun changes water in oceans and rivers into vapour, which rises into the atmosphere.

2. Water drains into rivers and then flows into lakes and oceans.

Cloud Spotting

Have you ever laid back, looked up at the clouds and picked out some of the weird and wonderful shapes they make? You might see a face, a car or even a sheep – and you probably know that clouds are an essential element of the planet's weather. They are giant, floating stores of water. Rain falls from warmer clouds near the Earth's surface. Cooler clouds, high in the atmosphere, produce hail and snow.

There are lots of different types of clouds floating above you. See if you can spot the four main categories of cloud:

Cloud Type	Cloud Clues	Cloud Shape
Cirrus	Long and wispy, like hair.	
Cumulus	Fluffy, with a flat base.	
Stratocumulus	Low-lying and grey in colour.	
Stratus	Low, layered sheets of cloud.	

Rain, Rain, Go Away!

Not everyone likes it when it rains, but it is essential to life on Earth. Plants and animals rely on it and humans use it for drinking, cooking, farming and washing.

How To Make A Raindrop

Making a raindrop requires certain ingredients. First, you need a large number of tiny particles, normally minute specks of sea salt, smoke particles or volcanic dust floating in the atmosphere.

Next, you need some water. This comes from rising warm air that cools as it moves higher in the atmosphere. As the air cools, water vapour in the air 'condenses', or turns to liquid. Water vapour can only condense into a liquid on a solid surface – you may have seen this at home, when you have a shower and the bathroom mirror steams up.

Similarly, up in the sky, minute cloud droplets condense on to the dust and salt particles. More and more water molecules gather on the particles, until they become too heavy and fall to Earth as rain.

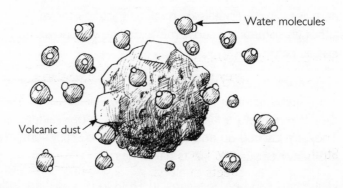

Water molecules

Volcanic dust

Somewhere Over The Rainbow

Sunlight is made up of lots of different colours, which you can see when a rainbow appears. The only things that nature needs to make a rainbow are sunlight and a rain shower. As the sunlight passes through the raindrops, each colour bends by a different amount, spreading it into a beautiful, colourful arc stretching across the sky.

Snow And Hail

Snowflakes are formed in the same way as rain but at much colder temperatures. When snow is formed, water vapour condenses directly into a solid, skipping the liquid phase entirely. It forms crystals around the tiny dust and ash particles. These crystals then fall to Earth as snow, although sometimes snow melts on the way down and falls as cold rain.

Hailstones are hard balls of ice that form when raindrops are driven high into the atmosphere by air currents. There, they freeze, before falling and collecting more raindrops. They are carried up and down on these currents until they are heavy enough to fall as hailstones.

Hailstones can be dangerous. In 1888 in Moradabad, India, hailstones the size of cricket balls fell, killing 250 people.

Thunder And Lightning

Thunderstorms start when warm, moist air meets colder air. The warm air is forced upwards, forming giant, towering clouds. Tiny ice crystals inside the clouds crash into each other, generating 'static electricity' (you may have done this by rubbing a balloon on a jumper). The top of the cloud becomes positively charged, while the bottom becomes negatively charged. Electricity crackles between the top and bottom of the cloud, shooting to the positively charged ground as lightning. The rumble or cracking sound of thunder is caused by the intense heat and expansion of air along the path of the lightning.

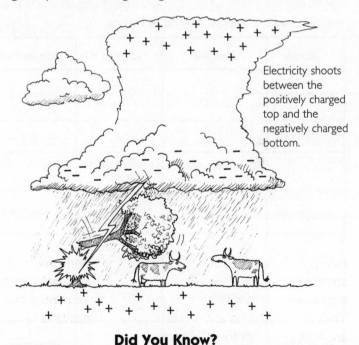

Electricity shoots between the positively charged top and the negatively charged bottom.

Did You Know?

Lightning bolts are less than 5cm wide but burn at a temperature that is hotter than the surface of the Sun.

Don't Blame It On The Meteorologist

You may have seen meteorologists, or weather forecasters, on the television, telling you what the weather will be like over the next few days. They might predict a thunderstorm for your day at the beach, or heavy snow on Christmas Day, leaving you disappointed when it only rains. You can't blame them for the weather when they are wrong though – meteorologists just study the weather – they don't make it.

Meteorologists look at lots of different elements of the weather and measure them using specialist equipment. They use this data to make predictions about the weather. To check out how and what meteorologists use to study the weather, take a look at the table below.

Element	Meaning	Measured In	Measured By
Temperature	How hot or cold it is	Degrees Celsius or Fahrenheit	Thermometer
Air pressure	How 'heavy' the air is	Millibars	Barometer
Cloud cover	How much of the sky is covered in cloud	Oktas, or eighths, of the sky	By sight or using satellite images
Wind speed	How fast the wind is blowing	Kilometres or miles per hour	Anemometer
Wind direction	The direction in which the wind is blowing	As a compass point, e.g. N, S etc.	Weather vane
Visibility	How far ahead you can see	Metres or kilometres	Visibility meter
Precipitation	Water falling from the sky, i.e. rain, snow and hail	Millilitres	Rain gauge

It's Getting Warmer

The delicate balance of the greenhouse effect (see page 28) is threatened by people burning huge quantities of natural oil and gas as fuel. You've probably heard people talk about 'global warming', but what does it mean, and how will it affect the planet?

Many people refer to the 'greenhouse effect' when they talk about global warming. What they actually mean is what is known as the 'enhanced greenhouse effect'. This is because the amount of greenhouse gases emitted into the atmosphere has increased massively in recent years.

Carbon dioxide is released when fuel is burned in power stations and for transport. Also, a gas called methane is released into the atmosphere by farm animals farting and burping. More of these gases in the atmosphere means that the Earth traps more heat and that average temperatures will increase. This is called global warming.

No one knows for sure how 'global warming' will affect the planet in the long term, but changes in weather patterns are being seen already. Deserts expand and flooding increases the more the planet's delicately balanced systems are disrupted.

A Cosy Blanket

You will have heard of the 'greenhouse effect' – it keeps the planet at the right temperature to support life. Gases, such as carbon dioxide and methane, are held in the atmosphere (the thin layer above the Earth's surface).

Greenhouse gases act as a blanket, trapping just the right amount of energy from the Sun during the day and releasing it at night, when it's cooler. This helps to maintain the fairly constant temperatures we have. For more on the greenhouse effect and global warming, see page 27.

Do You Recycle?

It could be said that Earth is one big recycling system. The next time you wonder if it's worth recycling your rubbish, think about how much recycling the planet does so you can live comfortably. Your own efforts to be a mini-recycling system help!

A Giant Recycling Ball

The Earth is an amazing planet, with lots of complex systems working together to support the many species that depend on it for life. These systems are delicately balanced to provide everything from the water we drink to the oxygen we breathe. Here are just a few of the amazing systems we rely on:

Heat and Light. When light from the Sun warms the Earth, the weather systems move the heat from the equator – an imaginary line around the middle of the Earth – towards the colder poles at the top and bottom. The deserts and oceans of the world soak up the Sun's heat and keep you warm, while the bright white clouds and icy poles reflect the Sun's rays and keep you cool. The Sun's rays also light the planet, allowing life to flourish.

Air and Food. Plant life across the Earth soaks up the carbon dioxide we breathe out. Plants use this to make sugars to help them grow. We consume many plants as food and medicines. Plants also give off the oxygen that we breathe.

Water. Did you know that water is constantly recycled (see page 21)? Much of the water you drink and wash in is the same water that ancient civilizations used.

THIS GLASS OF WATER HAS BEEN IN OUR FAMILY FOR GENERATIONS.

RIVERS AND LAKES

RAGING RIVERS

If you imagine Earth as a human body, then rivers would be the veins and the arteries that carry essential supplies from place to place. Rivers provide water for drinking, cooking, washing and farming, as well as acting as big, wet roads along which people can transport goods, or sail away to explore new lands. Throughout history, people have built their homes along the banks of rivers.

Where Do They Start?

One thing you can be certain of with rivers is that they all flow downhill, thanks to a force called 'gravity'. A river's starting point, or 'source', is high up, sometimes even on a mountain. Water from melting snow and rain trickles downwards, meeting other trickles and gathering up more water from rain as it flows, until it forms a stream. Sometimes, a stream bubbles up from the ground below as a spring. Streams flow quickly downhill, joining with other streams to become rivers. As land flattens out away from the hills and mountains, rivers usually flow at a slower pace than streams. The place where a river ends and flows out into a lake or ocean is called its 'mouth'.

Going With The Flow

Rivers don't just transport water and people as they flow from place to place – they are also the planet's very own earth-moving machines. Day and night, rivers are carving and smoothing the landscape. Each year, rivers erode and transport vast quantities of earth, or 'sediment'. The Ganges and the Brahmaputra in Asia are the Earth's biggest sediment-shifters.

Splash The C.A.S.H.

Actually, there are several different ways that rivers break rock and other materials down … that's where the 'C.A.S.H.' comes in:

Corrosion. The riverbed and banks are worn away by pebbles and stones carried along by the water.

Attrition. Rocks and stones wear each other down as they knock together in the moving water.

Solution. The river's water dissolves soluble minerals held in the riverbed and banks.

Hydraulic Action. The force of moving water breaks up the riverbed and banks.

The World's Longest Rivers

For centuries, geographers have argued over the length of the world's rivers. You might imagine that it would be a simple process to take a measuring tape and measure from the start of a river to its finish. In reality, the length of a river is very hard to calculate. This is because experts don't agree on the precise point at which some rivers start, nor on where exactly rivers finish and meet a lake or sea. As a result, the exact lengths of many rivers are hotly debated. One of the most fiercely fought battles is between the Nile and the Amazon over the title of 'The World's Longest River'. The following table shows you the longest rivers on each continent.

River	Continent	Length
Nile	Africa	6,693km
Amazon	South America	6,436km
Yangtze	Asia	6,300km
Mississippi	North America	6,275km
Volga	Europe	3,645km
Murray	Oceania	2,375km

River Deltas

At a river's mouth, the land is flatter, so it flows more slowly. The sediment it is carrying falls on to the banks and bed as 'deposits'. Over time, these deposits build up to form a triangular shape called a 'delta'. This is nature's way of extending an area of land.

The delta where the Ganges and the Brahmaputra end is the largest on the planet. It measures a whopping $100,000km^2$, and is home to more than 130 million people – that's double the entire population of the United Kingdom.

A river delta

... ER WHERE DO I MEASURE TO?

The sea

33

Wonderful Waterfalls

Waterfalls form when a river flows over layers of hard rock with softer rock underneath. Over hundreds of years, the water erodes the softer rock faster than the hard rock. This forms a vertical cliff with a plunge pool at the bottom.

Record-Breaking Falls

The following table shows six different waterfall records and which waterfall holds each one.

Highest Waterfall	Angel Falls, South America, 979m
Widest Curtain Of Water	Victoria Falls, Africa, 1.7km
Most Powerful In The World	Inǧa Falls, Africa, 70,793m³/sec
Most Powerful In North America	Niagara Falls, 8,269m³/sec
Tallest Man-Made Waterfall	Cascata delle Marmore Falls, Italy, 165m
Longest Run Of Waterfalls	Khone Falls, Laos, 12km

Some people have been crazy enough to take on the power of waterfalls with death-defying stunts. The most famous is Charles Blondin, who walked the tight-rope high above Niagara Falls in 1859. In 1901, Annie Edson Taylor went over the falls in a barrel, escaping unscathed. Others attempting the feat have not been so lucky...

Amazing Dams

For centuries, humans have built dams to store water and control river flow. The many dams built on rivers across the world store water for drinking in man-made lakes, which are called 'reservoirs'.

Dams are also used to control water flow to prevent flooding downstream. Many harness the power of water to turn turbines and generate electricity. The Niagara River is just one of many in the world where the power of the water has been harnessed to help humans. Incredibly, during the night and in the winter months, half of the flow of water from the Niagara River is diverted for hydro-electric power. One of the largest dams in the world is the Three Gorges Dam in China, spanning 2.3 kilometres.

Some people are concerned that dams may harm the environment. This is because they stop sediment from being carried downstream to create new land. In poorer countries, crops can fail downstream, due to reduced water flow, and many people can lose their homes when land is flooded to create dams.

Did You Know?

It's likely that people were inspired to build dams by watching animals called beavers that build dams for protection.

Flood!

Low-lying valleys are great places to live – most of the time. People have been drawn to live in them for thousands of years, thanks to their lush, fertile soil, and the rivers nearby, which are vital for drinking water, irrigation (supplying water for crops) and travel. The problem is, river valleys are vulnerable to flooding. This happens when a river overflows. It is a perfectly normal process for rivers – it helps to put nutrients in the soil, keeping it fertile. However, floods can be devastating for people living nearby. In fact, floods are the most commonly occurring natural hazard on the planet.

What Causes Floods?

There are many natural and man-made causes of flooding. Heavy rainfall can make a river burst its banks and overflow. Floods may be caused by the rapid melting of snow or even a man-made dam collapsing.

Where On Earth Does It Flood?

Your chance of being flooded depends on where you live on the planet. Historically, the worst place on Earth for flood risk is China. In the last 150 years, more than 5 million

people have been killed by floods. In the future, global warming (see page 27) means more people than ever will be vulnerable to the risk of flooding. Humans have covered huge areas of land in concrete and cut down trees. This means that water is washed more quickly into rivers, rather than soaking into the ground. If the climate warms, melting the polar ice caps, higher sea levels and more rain will mean larger areas of land will be affected by flooding.

Why Are Floods So Dangerous?

You've probably seen images of floods on television. These natural disasters can be very costly, not to mention dangerous. A powerful flood can sweep everything away, from rocks and trees to cars and houses. Foul-smelling water sweeps into buildings, and damages properties. On a bigger scale, everything from roads to crops and electricity lines may be destroyed. Although there's plenty of water around, you wouldn't want to drink it, as it's often contaminated with sewage and could make you very ill. Accessing food and clean water can be a real problem – that's if you can get somewhere safe and dry. Even when floodwater drains away, it can be months or even years before an area recovers.

GREAT LAKES

Lakes are found where rivers flow into hollows in the land. Not only are they lovely places to fish or swim, they also store 87 % of the world's fresh water found above ground. On a planet where 97 % of the water on the surface is salty and undrinkable, what's not to like about lakes?

How To Build A Lake

Several processes are responsible for creating holes in the ground in which water can collect. Some form in craters made by volcanic explosions or meteorites striking the Earth, but most lakes are formed thanks to a process known as glaciation. Here are the different ways a lake may form:

Glaciation. Glaciers are huge blocks of ice and snow that have built up over time. They creep very slowly down steep hills and mountains. As a glacier moves, millimetre by millimetre, it scrapes across the Earth's surface like a frozen earth-moving machine, digging out boulders, creating crevices and carving into the solid rock, or 'bedrock', that lies beneath the soil.

WHEN WILL THE LAKE BE READY, MUM?

Around 18,000 years ago, the Earth

was much colder than it is today and glaciers covered most of the land. They were continuously growing and moving. Later, as the Earth grew warmer and the 'Ice Age' ended, these vast blocks of ice began to melt. Over time, the glaciers' meltwaters filled the basins they had carved out, creating lakes. The world's largest freshwater lake system, North America's Great Lakes, was created in this way.

Tectonic Activity. This describes movements in the plates that make up the Earth's crust (see page 12). Tectonic activity can cause the crust to break into pieces and move apart, forming large holes in the ground called 'rift valleys'. When these holes fill with water, they form lakes. Lake Baikal in Siberia, Russia, was formed in this way. It is the world's deepest lake at 1,637 metres. It also contains the largest volume of fresh water on Earth.

Man-Made Lakes. People have built many artificial lakes or reservoirs (see page 35). For example, Lake Volta, in Ghana, has the largest surface area of a man-made lake. At 8,482km², it is roughly the same size as the French island of Corsica.

The Great Lakes Of North America

The Great Lakes is a system of five freshwater lakes situated in North America, on the border between Canada and the United States. The lakes are: Superior, Michigan, Huron, Erie and Ontario. Their shores are home to more than 33 million people. Together, the Great Lakes hold over 21% of the world's fresh water. In fact, if you were to pour out the water held in the lakes across the 48 states of mainland America, you'd create a gigantic swimming pool over 2.5 metres deep.

What Makes A Lake A Sea?

Did you know that not all lakes hold fresh water? Some lakes are saltier than the ocean. These are known as saltwater lakes. They are formed in the same way as freshwater lakes, but the thing that makes them different is that no water flows out of them. There is no outlet, such as a river, for the water to move to. This means that the only way that water can escape is by evaporating into the atmosphere as water vapour. When the water evaporates, it leaves salts and other minerals behind. As time goes by, the amount of salt in these lakes slowly builds up.

Saltwater lakes can be surrounded by land, so why are some of them known as seas? This was down to the ancient Romans, who decided that all large areas of salt water should be called seas. For example, the world's largest saltwater lake is the Caspian Sea, which is completely surrounded by land between Russia, Iran, Azerbaijan, Turkmenistan, and Kazakhstan.

Some lakes are really salty. The saltiest in the world is the Dead Sea in Israel. Almost nothing can live in the

Dead Sea's water, which is where the name comes from. However, another astonishing effect of all that extra salt is that you can float effortlessly in its waters!

Bleach-Filled Lakes

One of the strangest lakes in the world is found in Antarctica. Lake Untersee is Antarctica's largest freshwater lake, but its water isn't the kind anyone would want to drink. Thanks to some unusual chemical processes, it is more like the bleach used in a kitchen or bathroom. The freezing water of Lake Untersee is permanently covered with ice and is brimming with a gas called 'methane'.

Scientists have recently made an important discovery in Lake Untersee. Although it appeared that nothing could live in the bleach-like waters, they have found a group of minute organisms living there. Organisms that live in conditions too extreme for most forms of life are known as 'extremophiles'. They thrive in conditions too extreme for most other creatures. Some scientists are now suggesting that if species can exist in Lake Untersee's extreme conditions, there may be life in other places around the solar system, such as Mars and the moons of Jupiter and Saturn, which contain similar combinations of ice and methane.

OCEANS

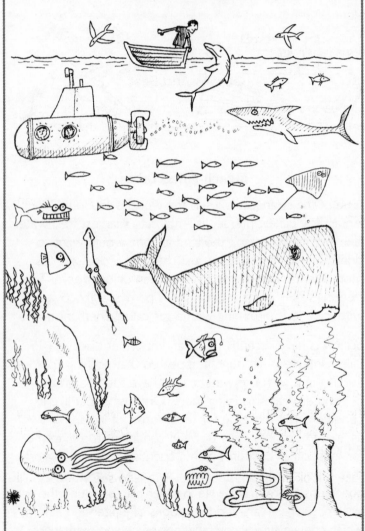

OCEANS IN MOTION

More than 70 % of the Earth's surface is covered by oceans. They are home to some of the deepest valleys and tallest mountains in the world. They can alter the Earth's weather and are jam-packed with life – yet much about them remains a mystery.

Oceans And Seas

The Earth's oceans are all connected and form one vast area of water, which is sometimes known as the global ocean. Usually, the global ocean is subdivided into five enormous oceans. In order of size, these are the Pacific, the Atlantic, the Indian, the Southern – or Antarctic – and the Arctic. An easy way to remember the names of the oceans is to use this saying:

I'm **A**bsolutely **S**pecific **A**bout the **P**acific

which stands for:

Indian, **A**tlantic, **S**outhern, **A**rctic and **P**acific.

The five oceans include many smaller subdivisions known as seas. Most are partly enclosed by land, but each sea is part of one of the oceans. One of the largest is the South China Sea in Asia. It is more than 3 million km^2, and is part of the Pacific Ocean. Some inland saltwater lakes, such as the Dead Sea, in Israel, are also called seas, because the water in them is so salty (see page 40).

Take a look at the table over the page to see where you'll find the Earth's oceans and how big they are.

Where On Earth Are The Oceans?

Ocean	Area	Where In The World?
Pacific	155,557,000km²	
Atlantic	76,762,000km²	
Indian	68,556,000km²	
Southern	20,327,000km²	
Arctic	14,056,000km²	

Hotter... Colder...

Oceans aren't just lovely for sailing on or swimming in, they work like a giant global thermostat, or temperature controller, regulating the planet's temperature.

Within the oceans are vast 'currents' of warm and cold water (a current is a movement of water). The currents determine how warm or cold ocean water is all over the world. Water in the oceans around the equator is warmed much more by the Sun than it is at the poles. Ocean currents continually move this warm water from the equator towards the colder regions at the poles, as shown here:

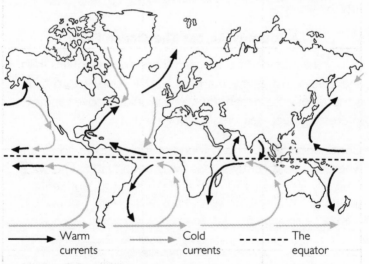

| ──────▶ Warm currents | ┈┈┈┈▷ Cold currents | ┈┈┈┈ The equator |

Warm ocean currents heat up the air above them as they travel. Cold ocean currents cool the air above them and move cold water away from polar regions towards the equator. This way, the ocean balances Earth's temperature – without them, the warmest parts of the planet would be much hotter, and the coldest parts would be even colder.

Not So Chilly Now

Cities in western Europe can be much warmer than cities in eastern North America, even if they are the same distance from the equator. Until recently, scientists believed that this was because of a current called the 'Gulf Stream'. However, in recent years, a team of scientists has shown that warm, westerly winds, which originate in the Rocky Mountains, have a much more important role in keeping western Europe warm.

This milder weather means that a winter in the United Kingdom usually isn't nearly as chilly as a winter in eastern North America.

A Journey Across The Ocean Floor

Below the surface of the ocean there are mountains, hills and valleys, just as there are on land. If you were to take a trip across the ocean floor, you would discover some interesting deep-sea details along the way:

Continental Shelf. This is found at the edges of continents, where the land gently slopes away underwater. The water is usually less than 130 metres deep along a continental shelf.

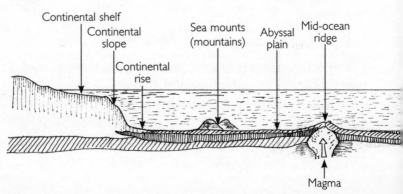

Continental shelf
Continental slope
Continental rise
Sea mounts (mountains)
Abyssal plain
Mid-ocean ridge
Magma

Continental Slope. At the edge of a continental shelf, the land slopes more steeply towards the ocean floor.

Continental Rise. Right at the foot of a continental slope is a gentle hill formed by built-up sediment. This leads to the deep ocean.

Abyssal Plains. This forms most of the ocean's floor. It can be up to 5,000 metres deep and forms the smooth floor of the deep ocean. Abyssal Plains are continuously being covered by a thick sediment.

Sea Mounts. These are tall, solitary mountains that rise at least 1,000 metres from the seaf loor.

Mid-Ocean Ridges. Across the ocean floor, long chains of underwater mountains have been found in an almost continuous chain around the world. The ridges form where two tectonic plates are moving apart. Magma from inside the Earth erupts as lava to build these underwater mountains.

Deep-Sea Trench. The deepest points of an ocean floor can be more than 11,000 metres below the surface.

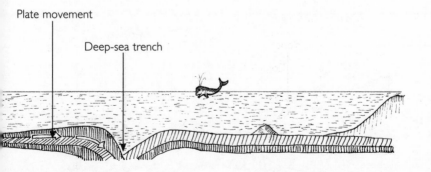

Plate movement

Deep-sea trench

Mountain High, Valley Low

If you could drain the water from all of the Earth's oceans, you would be able to see an incredible landscape with the highest mountains and deepest valleys on the planet.

Mauna Kea is a volcano in the Pacific Ocean. It is one of five volcanos that together form the island of Hawaii (the largest in the Hawaiian island chain). Mauna Kea stands at 4,205 metres tall. This makes it much lower than Mount Everest, which, at 8,848 metres, is generally thought to be the tallest mountain on Earth.

There's a catch though. The geographers who put together these figures measure the height of a mountain from sea level and work up. This puts Mauna Kea at a distinct disadvantage as most of it is underwater. If the height of Mauna Kea was measured from its base on the ocean floor, it would be more than 10,000 metres tall – which would make it the world's tallest mountain.

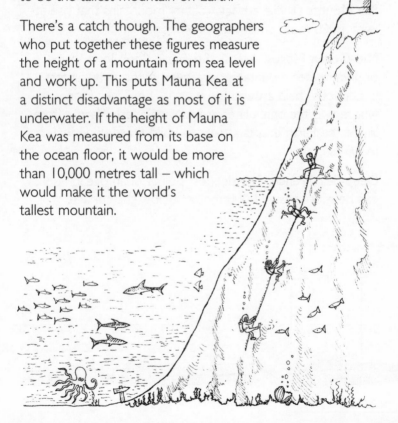

Whoah, That's Deep!

The Pacific Ocean is also where you can find the deepest point on the planet – the Mariana Trench. Within this lies a valley called Challenger Deep, which, at nearly 11,000 metres below sea level, is thought to be one of the deepest points on Earth. To put it another way, if you picked up Mount Everest and dropped it into Challenger Deep, Everest's peak would still be 3,000 metres underwater!

Under Pressure

Scientists are keen to discover more about the ocean floor, but exploring the deep ocean can be even more dangerous than going into space. As you dive underwater, the weight of the water above you increases the pressure. At great depths, the pressure is so much that you would be crushed to death unless you were in a specially adapted submarine. That's not all. In the lower zones of the ocean, it is pitch black and very cold, as the Sun's rays can't travel that far. There are pockets of very high temperatures, however, caused by holes in the ocean floor called 'hydrothermal vents', which spew out red-hot liquids and gases.

What could be worth such a dangerous journey? Well, there are still some amazing features and creatures to be discovered on the ocean floor. In the depths of the oceans, life is very different. Scientists have discovered many creatures, such as giant deep-sea clams, that get their energy from deep sea vents instead of the Sun. Animals that can survive with no sunlight, at extreme temperatures and bone-crushing pressures, help people to understand the planet better. The fact that creatures have adapted to these extreme conditions makes some scientists believe that there may be life on other planets within the solar system.

Crazy Coastlines

The coast is a narrow strip of land that borders the sea along a continent or an island. Coastlines are battered by wind and sea, which constantly changes and shapes the land to create some very unusual landforms.

Waves are the busiest sculptors on the coastline. They are built up by winds far out at sea, then unleash their energy when they break on the shore. The strength of the wind blowing over the ocean has a direct impact on how big or small waves will be.

On a beach, the inward rush of a wave is called the 'swash'. It carries sand, gravel and pebbles on to the beach. As the wave retreats down the beach, the 'backwash' carries sand and gravel out to sea. Since waves usually hit the beach at an angle, but always go straight out, the waves gradually move sand and gravel along the beach in a process known as 'longshore drift'.

Fetch!

At Miami Beach, longshore drift means that, without humans taking action, the beach would not exist any more,

because the sand from the beach gets carried up the coast. Every five years or so, sand is moved back down the beach to replenish the areas where it has been carried away.

Life's A Beach

For hundreds of years, people have flocked to the coast to relax and do water sports, but will these beaches exist in the future? They are under threat from two things: coastal erosion and rising sea levels (sea levels rise as the oceans get warmer and polar ice melts). In some areas, such as low-lying islands in the Pacific, a one-metre rise in sea levels would be catastrophic. Florida's Everglades in the USA could be completely submerged. Low-lying countries, such as Bangladesh and the Netherlands, are also at risk, as are parts of southeast England.

If this happened, the world map could look very different, with the shape of some countries and continents changed for ever – some low-lying islands could disappear from the map completely.

MOUNTAINS

GOING UP!

Planet Earth's mountain ranges are jagged towers of rock that rise high into the skies. They are formed by processes that take place deep below the Earth's surface.

How Do Mountains Climb?

There are four main ways in which mountains form:

Folds. This is the most common way for mountains to form – the Himalayas in Asia were created in this way. Mountains form when two continental plates crash into one another, causing the crust to crumple, pushing land up.

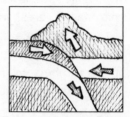

Eruptions. Repeated volcanic eruptions along areas where the continental plates meet, called faults, can cause molten rock and ash to spew out from inside the Earth. These substances build up over time to form mountains.

Faults. This process also takes place along the fault lines. Sometimes, when two plates push together, instead of folding, they crack and a huge chunk of rock is pushed up to create what is known as a 'block mountain'.

Domes. These form when magma, or 'molten rock', in the mantle increases in pressure, pushing the Earth's crust up from below. This process makes rounded, dome-shaped mountains.

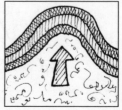

The Sky's The Limit

Did you know that some mountains are still growing?
Evidence has been found that some mountains used to be
at, or even below, sea level. Rock samples from mountain
ranges, such as the Himalayas and the Andes, have been
found to contain sea shells dating back over 18,000 years.

As plates are continually shifting, the world will continue
to change. Scientists believe that the world's highest
mountain, Everest, in the Himalayas, is still growing and
is also shifting in a north-easterly direction. Currently
measured at 8,848 metres, it is possible that Everest's
future climbers will have a longer trek to the top
than those who reached its summit in the past.

Wear And Tear

Before a mountain has finished growing, wind,
water and ice set to work, wearing it
down in a process called erosion.
This is responsible for the wide
variety of mountain shapes
you can see today.

SURELY THIS
MUST BE
THE TOP?

Ice, in the form of glaciers (see page 38) creates some of the most eye-catching mountain features by carving deep into the rock. Here are some of the main features carved by glaciers:

Cirques. These bowl-shaped hollows form in the side of a mountain and are also known as 'corries' or 'cwms'. They are caused by an enormous glacier carving rock from the steep mountain wall, scouring a hollow into the land below as the rocky debris rotates in the ice above.

Arêtes. These are thin ridges, which are created when cirques form on opposite sides of a mountain. As the glaciers erode, the mountain ridge between them gets narrower and narrower.

Pyramidal Peaks. These are also known as 'glacial horns'. They are created when three or more cirques form on different sides of a mountain, leaving very jagged peaks. The Matterhorn, in the Alps, was formed in this way.

Glacial ice carves away the rock.

Cirque

Glacier

Rocky debris scours away the base, forming a hollow.

A lip forms as some debris is deposited at the edge of the cirque.

The World's Tallest Mountains

Use this table to check the heights of the tallest mountains on each continent:

Mountain	Continent	Height Above Sea Level
Everest	Asia	8,848 metres
Aconcagua	South America	6,962 metres
Mount McKinley	North America	6,190 metres
Kilimanjaro	Africa	5,895 metres
Elbrus	Europe	5,642 metres
Vinson Massif	Antarctica	4,890 metres
Puncak Jaya	Oceania	4,884 metres

Use this clever trick to remember the seven summits:

PEAK V ME:
Puncak Jaya, **E**verest, **A**concagua, **K**ilimanjaro, **V**inson Massif, **M**cKinley and **E**lbrus.

Some scientists argue that Oceania's highest peak should be Australia's Mount Kosciuszco, as Puncak Jaya (see above) is in New Guinea, and although it is part of the Australian continental shelf, it actually belongs to Asia. As no one can reach an agreement, some intrepid folk who want to climb the seven highest mountains in the world have ended up climbing both, just to be sure!

Mountain Dangers

Mountains are very exciting places, but they can be very dangerous, too. Read on to discover the perils to be found in the peaks.

Altitude Sickness. Human beings need to breathe oxygen to survive. As mountain climbers reach higher altitudes, the air becomes much thinner and there is less oxygen. When climbers' bodies are unable to adjust to there being less oxygen, they may get altitude sickness, which can lead to tiredness, confusion, vomiting and even death.

To prevent altitude sickness, climbers must avoid going too high too fast. They are advised to climb in stages, stopping for up to three days at a time, to allow their bodies to get used to the lower levels of oxygen.

Snow Blindness. This is caused by 'ultraviolet', or UV, radiation. At lower altitudes, a lot of UV radiation is filtered out by the atmosphere, but it can still cause a nasty case of sunburn. At higher altitudes, there is less atmosphere and more UV radiation because less is filtered out. The bright, white sheets of snow and ice on a mountain increase the effect of the UV radiation by reflecting up to 80% of it, some of which will bounce into a climber's eyes. Snow blindness leaves the eyes feeling sore and as though they have grit in them, as they are burned by the light. Eyelids may swell so much that they will not open. Usually the effects are temporary and the eyes recover. Snow blindness can be prevented by wearing UV-filtering sunglasses.

Frostbite. Frostbite is caused when climbers get so cold that their bodies stop sending blood to the areas furthest away from their hearts, particularly their fingers and toes. The body does this to protect the climbers' vital internal organs. When this happens, the affected parts begin to freeze. Frostbite will cause climbers' fingers and toes to tingle and itch and then feel numb. If left untreated the affected areas may become so badly damaged that they need to be removed. Yuck!

Climbers can prevent frostbite by wearing protective, warm clothing and by eating high-energy foods and warm drinks.

Avalanches

Wherever there is lots and lots of snow and a slope it is quite possible that there will be an 'avalanche' – a large amount of snow and ice sliding down the side of a mountain at speeds of up to 200km/hr.

Snow builds up on a mountainside in layers. The layers of snow are not stable – snow may freeze and thaw, forming ice layers, and also be packed tightly or loosely. As more snow builds up on a steep slope the danger of vast amounts of snow sliding down the mountain increases, meaning that an avalanche may happen at any time.

Avalanches can be triggered by lots of different things – slope steepness, very heavy snowfall, an increase in temperature, rain, an earthquake or even the vibrations caused by heavy traffic nearby. Sometimes they can be caused by skiers who have ventured off the ski slopes. When an avalanche is triggered, many tonnes of snow begin to slide down the mountain, gathering speed. If you are in the path of an avalanche, your chances of survival aren't good. The average speed of an avalanche is around 40–60km/h, but they can be much faster. They will tear up trees, block roads and bury everything and everyone in their path. In mountainous areas, explosives are sometimes used to create controlled mini-avalanches, to ensure that snow doesn't build up to dangerous levels.

Snow Joke!

Did you know that elephants have climbed mountains? In 218 BCE, a military commander called Hannibal crossed Europe's Alps, to fight the Romans. As well as his army, he had horses and elephants to carry supplies. Many lost their lives on the journey, thanks to fierce avalanches in the snowy peaks.

COLD POLES

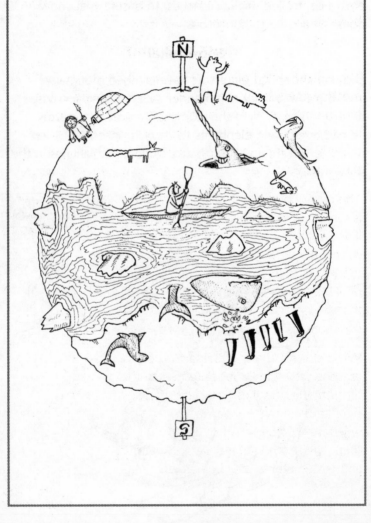

IT'S FREEZING!

What's so exciting about the polar regions – the two enormous frozen wastelands at the top and bottom of the planet? There's nothing but ice and snow for as far as your eyes can see – except for the odd seal, penguin or polar bear. Surely the poles are exactly the same? Wrong!

North Or South?

The exact North Pole, located in the Arctic Circle, is the most northerly point on the planet. If you stood at the North Pole and walked in any direction, you would be heading south. At the North Pole, and the area around it, there is no land at all. What explorers are walking on when they attempt to reach it is hundreds of kilometres of ice.

The exact South Pole, located in the Antarctic, is the most southerly point on the planet. If you stood at the South Pole and walked in any direction, you would be heading north. Unlike the North Pole, the South Pole is located on land, but it's buried under ice more than two kilometres deep. Antarctica is a continent almost twice the size of Australia.

What else sets the poles apart? Their seasons are entirely opposite due to the tilt of the Earth's axis (see page 19). So on a balmy summer's day in the Arctic, when it might be as warm as 0°C, it's a teeth-chattering winter's day in Antarctica and temperatures could be as low as −49°C.

It's Been A Long Day ...

Did you know that at the North and South Poles, a summer day can last up to six months and a winter's night can be just as long? This is because the Earth spins at an angle (see page 19). As the Earth spins, the top of the planet, the North Pole, points at the Sun for six months and then points away from it for the next six months. This means that when the Arctic is bathed in summer sunshine, the Antarctic is plunged into a long, dark winter, and vice versa.

Even though the poles get so many hours of sunshine, their summers are still very cold and temperatures rarely climb above 0°C. This is because the Sun is always low in the sky and its rays are weakened as they have to travel further to reach the poles than they do to reach the equator. The poles are also covered in white ice, which reflects heat back into the atmosphere.

Planet Earth's Designer Sunglasses

Believe it or not, the ice, snow and freezing temperatures at the planet's poles help keep the rest of the world at a comfortable temperature range.

The icy poles are bright white in colour and this maximizes their 'albedo'. The word 'albedo' (pronounced 'al-bee-doh') is used to describe how reflective the surfaces on Earth are.

Earth's oceans and dark soils aren't very good at reflecting the Sun's rays, so they have a very low albedo – about 10 %. This means they absorb more heat from the Sun than they reflect. Fresh snow has a high albedo – around 85% or more. So large, icy areas like the North and South Poles act like giant mirrors, reflecting most of the sunlight they receive back into space, helping the planet stay cool. If there were no ice at the Earth's poles, the planet would be a much warmer place.

Bright Lights In The Long Nights

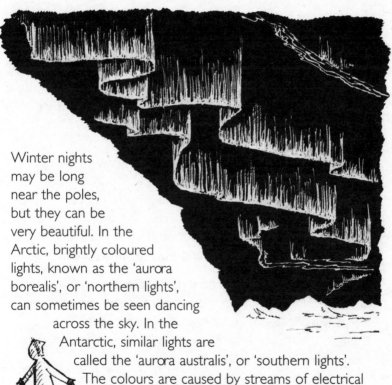

Winter nights may be long near the poles, but they can be very beautiful. In the Arctic, brightly coloured lights, known as the 'aurora borealis', or 'northern lights', can sometimes be seen dancing across the sky. In the Antarctic, similar lights are called the 'aurora australis', or 'southern lights'. The colours are caused by streams of electrical particles from space clashing with the Earth's atmosphere. Long ago, many people believed that these lights were dangerous!

The 'Warm' Pole

The Arctic is the 'warmer' of the two poles. Its temperature ranges from 0°C in the summer to a very cold −30°C in the winter. The Antarctic is much colder. The average summer temperature there is around −30°C, and in the winter it can reach below −60°C. The coldest temperature ever recorded on Earth was −89°C at Vostok station, Antarctica, in July 1983.

Did You Know?

Until recently, many explorers and scientists thought the Arctic, like Antarctica, was an ice-covered continent. In 1958, a submarine journeyed beneath the ice cap and came out the other side, proving that the Arctic is nothing but ice.

A Deserted Desert

When you visit a foreign country, a good way of learning about it is by talking to the local people. You can't do that in Antarctica. Antarctica has no 'indigenous' people – which is a clever way of saying 'locals'. There are a few thousand research scientists who have set up bases to study there, but no one else lives there, and you can understand why.

Not only is the Antarctic dark for six months of the year and the coldest place on the planet, it is also the windiest and driest. Antarctica is technically a frozen desert. It is thought that in some spots, such as McMurdo Sound, rain hasn't fallen for more than two million years!

Polar Bear Versus Penguin

You may have seen polar bears and penguins sitting happily together on Christmas cards, but these polar survivors are never likely to meet.

Polar bears live in the Arctic, and penguins live in the Antarctic and parts of the southern hemisphere, but which is the toughest?

The Polar Bear. This is the largest meat-eater living on land. It is well-suited to sub-zero temperatures, and can travel over snow and ice easily. The polar bear is a great swimmer, too. It has a thick layer of fat beneath its skin, which acts like thermal underwear to keep it warm and to help it float in icy water. It is also armed with powerful jaws and large claws, and it can smell prey over great distances. The polar bear has to survive winter temperatures of −30°C in the Arctic, but that's nothing …

The Penguin. The Emperor penguin is the largest species of penguin. Like the polar bear, it is a super swimmer and has a thick layer of fat under its skin to keep it warm. However, that's not what makes it the winner of this polar contest. The Emperor penguin breeds during the bone-chilling Antarctic winter. While the female penguin goes in search of food, the male is left behind to  protect their egg through the harshest winter on Earth. He faces temperatures of −60°C, fierce winds and four months without sunlight, food or water. He huddles with other males on the polar ice, waiting for the mother penguin to return and take over feeding the chick. That puts the penguin in 'pole' position in this contest.

ISLANDS

WE'RE SURROUNDED!

Landing on a beautiful island paradise would make for a heavenly holiday. Planet Earth has more than 100,000 islands, so there are plenty to choose from, but what makes an island an island, and how did they form?

The World's Biggest Island

Deciding which is the world's biggest island should be easy. Surely all you need to do is look at a map or a globe and pick out the largest area of land that's totally surrounded by water? Well, it's not that simple. You could be fooled into thinking that the world's biggest island is Australia. It sits on its own, surrounded by ocean and is more than three times the size of its nearest rival Greenland.

However, geographers have decided that there has to be a cut-off point between islands and continents. Australia is often classed as a continent, bouncing it out of the top spot for biggest island. In this book, it is included as part of Oceania (see pages 114 to 121). This leaves Greenland, which covers an area of 2,175,600km², to claim the title.

Making Islands

Greenland was once part of North America, so how did it become an island? Here is how the two main types of island form:

Continental Islands. These islands are part of a continent that has been flooded so that only the highest points lie above sea level, creating islands. Most continental islands were formed at the end of the last Ice Age, when huge glaciers covering the land melted. The vast amounts of meltwater flowing into the oceans made sea levels rise, flooding low-lying areas at the edges of the land. This happened in Norway in northern Europe, creating over 3,000 islands along its rugged coast.

The British Isles and Greenland are also continental islands on a much larger scale. If sea levels fell far enough, Britain would be reconnected with Europe. This would mean that people couldn't swim the Channel any more, but they could walk across to pick up a fresh croissant and a baguette or two from France.

Oceanic Islands. The Earth's crust is a jigsaw of moving pieces called tectonic plates (see page 12). Oceanic islands are formed by volcanic activity along the edges of these plates on the ocean floor. Where plates are moving apart from each other, the Earth's crust cracks, allowing hot, melted rock, known as magma, to bubble up, forming an undersea volcano. The magma cools and solidifies. Eventually, the volcano grows so high that it rises above sea level, forming an island. Easter Island in the Pacific was formed this way.

Oceanic islands are also formed where one plate slips underneath the other. As the crust is pushed into the mantle, it melts and turns into magma. This erupts to form a chain of islands, known as an 'island arc'. This is how the Aleutian Islands, situated at the northern edge of the Pacific, were created.

Hot Spots. Hot spots are super-heated places deep inside the Earth. They are so hot that they can melt the Earth's crust, allowing lava to burst through to form volcanoes. This lava builds over time until the volcano is tall enough to break through the surface of the sea. Surtsey Island in the Atlantic is an example of this kind of oceanic island.

Hot spots build islands hundreds of kilometres away from tectonic plate boundaries. Over millions of years, a single hot spot can build a whole chain of islands. This is because a hot spot stays put as the tectonic plate above slowly moves over it. As the plate moves, the hot spot melts new holes in the crust, creating new volcanoes and new islands.

The southeastern
Hawaiian Islands

The Hawaiian Island chain was created in this way. There are 132 Hawaiian islands, and the newest is being built right now at the bottom of the Pacific Ocean. Don't book a holiday there just yet – it will take tens of thousands of years for this little lump of lava to show its face above the surface.

We're Not An Island Atoll

Once a new volcanic island has drifted away from the hot spot that created it, it starts to sink. Rain, wind and waves wear the island away until it disappears below the surface for ever. The Hawaiian islands run from the oldest islands in the northwest to the youngest in the southeast of the Pacific. The oldest and most remote Hawaiian island is not an island at all … it used to be, but now it's just an 'atoll'. An atoll is formed when a coral reef grows around a volcanic island. As the coral reef grows, the volcanic island is eroded away, eventually leaving a ring of coral with shallow water or a 'lagoon' in the middle.

Did You Know?

Coral is formed from the hard skeletons left behind by tiny creatures called polyps, so atolls are actually built by tiny animals.

Getting There

As far as people know, there has never been a wild cat or a kangaroo captaining a boat. If islands are completely surrounded by water, how did the plants and animals that live on them get there?

By Land. Continental islands were once part of the larger continent before sea levels rose. Animals and plants that happened to be on the land that got separated from the continent got stuck there for ever.

By Sea. Getting to an oceanic island is much more of an adventure. Insects, spiders, snakes and snails can set sail aboard chunks of driftwood. These tiny intrepid travellers walk, scuttle or slither on to pieces of wood that are washed away then go where the ocean currents take them. They end up on new islands where they'll settle and reproduce.

Plants can travel by sea, too. Nuts with thick, well-armoured shells, such as coconuts, can drop into water and float to new lands. When they arrive, they often sprout, bringing new plants and trees to an island.

By Air. Ready for take off? Obviously, many types of birds and insects can fly. It's easy to see how they could make it to islands. However, did you know that plants have also taken to the skies? Sticky seeds get stuck to birds' feathers and fall off whenever the birds land, and grow in the new soil. Other seeds are eaten by birds and are 'dropped off' in their droppings. These seeds have the benefit of landing with their very own fertilizer. Lots of seeds can also be blown over to islands from other places by the winds.

Did You Know?

People can make their very own islands from scratch, too! The Palm Islands in Dubai are three giant, man-made islands in the shape of palm trees, each surrounded by a crescent island.

The islands, named Jumeirah, Jebel Ali and Deira, are home to expensive hotels and luxury apartments as well as restaurants, shops and leisure facilities. Construction is still ongoing, but the Palm Islands will add 520 kilometres of beach front to the city of Dubai.

DESERTS

DESERTS DEFINED

When you mention the word 'desert', almost everyone imagines a scorching hot, sandy place filled with camels and palm trees. Actually, hot, sandy deserts only make up about a quarter of the deserts on planet Earth.

Geographers define a desert as an area of land that receives less than 25cm of rain or snow per year, or loses more moisture by evaporation or 'transpiration' – the moisture given off by plants – than it receives.

This means that a place can't be classed as a desert just because of high temperatures. In fact, planet Earth is home to many cold deserts, as well as hot ones, and they're found on every continent – even Antarctica!

Life In A Hot Desert

Trying to survive in a hot desert is very tough. In the British Isles, the hottest temperature ever recorded was just above 36°C. On a sunny day in a desert such as the Sahara, the temperature can climb above 50°C and fall to below 0°C at night. With extreme temperatures like this, people, plants and animals can find it very difficult to survive.

Danger In The Dunes

Some deserts may look like the perfect places to grab a bucket and start building the most awesome sandcastle ever, but beware, deserts can be deadly. Here's why:

Dehydration. This occurs when people haven't drunk enough water, so their bodies lose more water than they are taking in. Scorching temperatures can cause people to sweat a lot, which increases water loss. Dehydration can be serious, and lead to confusion, loss of direction, and even death. Desert travellers need to drink up to 10 litres of water a day to stay alive.

Hyperthermia. This is caused by a person's body temperature getting so high that it just can't cool itself down. Hyperthermia can cause headaches, dizziness and cramps, and it can be fatal. To prevent hyperthermia, desert travellers need to avoid travelling during the hottest times of the day, drink plenty of water, wear lightweight cotton clothing and a hat, and spend as much time in the shade as they can.

Desert Dwellers

The Bedouin people of North Africa have adapted to survive in the desert. They live in cool, shady tents and lead a nomadic life, travelling from place to place looking for food and water with their animals. They wear long, flowing robes that let the air move around their bodies. This keeps them cool as well as protecting them from the Sun.

Did You Know?

There are two species of camel. The dromedary has one hump and the bactrian camel has two humps. Camels store fat in their humps to use for energy. This means they can go for days without food.

Aborigines

Aborigines, the indigenous people of Australia, traditionally live in the dry and dusty centre of Australia, called the

Outback. They have some truly ingenious ways of surviving in the desert. Like the Bedouin, Aborigines travel around looking for food and water, and are experts at tracking animals, hunting kangaroos and other creatures with spears and boomerangs. They have also become experts at foraging for 'bush-tucker', such as berries, nuts and insects, including witchetty grubs, which are eaten raw and wriggling!

Deserts Bite

Deserts are home to some of the most venomous animals on Earth – snakes and scorpions.

The death-stalker scorpion is found in deserts in North Africa and the Middle East. It is up to 11cm long and packs a powerful sting in its tail. This can cause a deadly allergic reaction that can kill.

Of the ten deadliest snakes in the world, six are found in Australia, including the inland taipan, which is also known as the 'fierce snake'. This has been classified as the most venomous land snake on the planet. A single bite can kill in just 45 minutes.

How Do Deserts Form?

Deserts come in all shapes and sizes – and they are formed in different ways and in a variety of places, from coastal areas to the middle of giant continents. Here's how:

Trade Wind Deserts. The trade winds blow air towards the equator, where it heats up and rises, moving away from the equator once more. As the air cools, rain falls. By the time the air reaches the edges of the tropics (see page 18) it is dry again, so little rain falls. Most of the world's deserts are trade wind deserts. The world's largest hot desert, the Sahara is a trade wind desert. Temperatures there can be as high as 57°C.

Coastal Deserts. These deserts are created where there are cold ocean currents. The air doesn't take up as much moisture as it would over warm waters, so there is less rain. The Atacama in South America is a coastal desert. Some geographers claim that there are parts of the Atacama desert where no rain has ever fallen.

Rain-Shadow Deserts. When rain-filled clouds pass over mountain ranges, they are forced to rise. The air cools and rain or snow falls. A desert is formed in the rain 'shadow' on the other side of the range because there is little or no rain left to fall there.

Montane Deserts. These deserts are found in areas higher than 3,000 metres above sea level. These places have average annual rainfall of less than 4cm a year as so few clouds ever reach them. One of the best-known examples of a montane desert can be found in northern Tibet.

Inland Deserts. These deserts are found near the centre of continents, far away from oceans. Clouds are formed over oceans and as they move inland the air rises and cools, and the clouds produce rain. On large continents, the rain has fallen long before winds reach the centre. The Gobi Desert, in Mongolia, is a typical inland desert.

Polar Deserts. Even though polar deserts might be covered in ice and snow, annual precipitation in these teeth-chatteringly cold places is less than 25cm a year, which makes them deserts. The Antarctic desert is an example of a polar desert. In some parts of Antarctica, it is estimated that rain hasn't fallen for more than two million years!

The World's Largest Deserts

The chart below shows planet Earth's top deserts in order of size:

Desert	Continent	Size
Antarctic Desert	Antarctica	14,000,000km^2
Sahara	Africa	8,600,000km^2
Arabian Desert	Asia	2,330,000km^2
Gobi Desert	Asia	1,300,000km^2
Kalahari Desert	Africa	930,000km^2

Desert Disaster

Did you know that the desert regions of Earth are growing and that new ones are being created? The growth of desert areas is due to a process called 'desertification'. This process is being speeded up by:

Farming. There are more people on the planet today than ever before, and they need to be fed. This means more land is needed to grow crops and raise cattle, so more forest is cleared and land that isn't suitable for farming is now being cultivated.

Across the globe, demand for meat is constantly increasing. This means that the world's crops are being used less efficiently. Nearly 40% of the world's grain is fed to cattle, whose meat feeds fewer people than the grain would have.

Poor Soil Conservation. In some areas where there is hardly any rain, intensive farming can lead to soil 'degradation'. When soil degrades, it gets broken up and topsoil is washed or gets blown away. Plants no longer grow as the land is no longer fertile.

Deforestation. Where a forest is cleared for grazing, or trees are cut down for firewood, the topsoil is eroded as it is no longer held in place by the trees' roots. Also, a bare area of land increases the amount of heat reflected back into the atmosphere and the amount of water lost to evaporation, as there are no plants to hold water. This makes the area even drier.

FORESTS

FORESTS

Forests are filled with plants and animals that are essential for keeping humans alive. About 30% of the Earth's land surface is covered by lush green forest that is vital for sustaining life on Earth.

Pollution Filters

A forest is defined as a large area covered by trees. Forests are often described as the world's pollution filters. This is because they are able to absorb billions of tonnes of carbon dioxide. This is important because carbon dioxide is one of the greenhouse gases thought to be causing global warming. It is produced by cars and factories, but also by humans and animals just breathing out!

All the different kinds of plants in forests take the carbon in the air (carbon dioxide is made up of carbon and oxygen), combine it with water in a chemical reaction powered by sunlight, and turn it into sugar for food. The waste products of this process are water and oxygen – the gas you need to breathe. This process is called 'photosynthesis'.

Water

Types Of Forest

Forests can be found on every single continent, except Antarctica. They grow almost everywhere – from the hot and steamy areas around the equator, to the frosty lands of North America, Europe and Asia. Read on to find out about some of the different types of forest.

Temperate Forests. These are found in areas where temperatures are fairly moderate, and soils are rich. Temperate forests are mostly made up of 'deciduous' trees, such as oak, ash and maple. In autumn, deciduous trees lose their leaves, remaining bare during winter. Around 5,000 years ago, most of the British Isles was covered by forests, but many were cleared as humans began to use the land to cultivate crops and keep animals.

Boreal Forests. These are found in the cooler northern areas of North America, Europe and Asia. Boreal forests are made up of different types of 'coniferous' tree. Coniferous trees, such as pine and spruce, are cone-shaped, which allows snow to slide off them easily. Coniferous trees keep their needle-like leaves all year round, so they are known as evergreen trees. Many species grow to record-breaking heights. In California, a coast redwood called Hyperion stands at a colossal 115 metres!

Tropical Rainforests. These are found in tropical areas around the equator, in Africa, Asia, South America and Australia. Rainforests are warm all year round and are teeming with life.

Rainforest Layers

It is estimated that rainforests are home to about half of the planet's plant and animal species.

There is so much competition for light and space in the rainforest that plants and animals have adapted to living in different layers.

The Rainforest. This scene shows a typical rainforest with four layers. Trees and plants need light and space to grow.

The Understorey Layer. There is very little light in this layer. There are vines, called 'lianas', growing around the trees and small ferns and shrubs. It is also home to many insects, spiders and reptiles, as well as small mammals.

The Forest Floor. This layer is very damp and dark. It is also home to a mind-boggling variety of creatures, from spiders to pigs and deer to big cats.

The Emergent Layer. In this layer the tops of the tallest trees, such as mahogany, tower above the canopy. These trees are at the mercy of strong winds and sunlight. This layer is home to many birds and insects.

The Canopy. Sometimes known as the 'umbrella', this tangled layer of dense branches is rich in life, from flowers and fruits to monkeys and birds. It is so thick that it blocks out virtually all light for the vegetation below.

Forest Fun Facts And 'Tree-Via'

• Until recently, it was thought that the oldest tree in the world was a 4,700-year-old bristlecone pine named 'Methuselah', growing in California, USA. Recently, scientists have found a spruce tree in Sweden, which they believe has been growing for nearly 10,000 years!

• The Amazon rainforest covers an area of around 6 million km² and stretches through nine countries in South America. The rainforest is so big that it is believed that there may still be people living in the forest who have never had contact with the outside world.

• The titan arum grows in the rainforests of Indonesia. It is the world's largest flower, growing up to 3 metres tall and 1.5 metres across. This isn't one to buy for your mum, as it's said to smell like rotting meat and dead bodies – yuck!

• Chewing gum used to be made from the sap of spruce trees. The ancient Mayans used to chew the sap of sapodilla trees which are found in the rainforests of Central America.

The Future Of Forests

In the last 50 years, more than a fifth of the Amazon rainforest has been destroyed. People cut the trees to sell the wood for building homes or making furniture, or to clear the land to grow crops and graze cattle. This affects the planet in many ways.

Extinction. About half of all the species of plants and animals on Earth live in rainforests. Cutting down the forest means that these species have nowhere to live and die out. Scientists believe that the planet is losing up to 50 species each day, many of them from rainforests. If animals and plants are wiped out, others that depend on them to survive will also die out.

Humans use many plant species found in the rainforest to make medicines. Destroying these species means that the chance to find a cure for some diseases may also be lost.

Global Warming. Cutting down forests also speeds up global warming, as the Earth's forests absorb billions of tonnes of carbon dioxide gas each year. This includes 30% of the carbon dioxide humans put into the air with their cars and power stations. As areas of forest are destroyed, there are fewer trees to absorb the carbon dioxide. Carbon dioxide is a greenhouse gas, and the more greenhouse gas there is in the atmosphere, the warmer the planet gets (see pages 27 to 28).

Desertification. The trees and plants in forests hold the soil together and stop it from blowing or washing away. Cutting down forests means that more soil is exposed to the wind and rain, which can lead to areas becoming deserts (see page 80).

There are ways to conserve the forests and plant new ones. Conservationists are urging people to treat forests with respect, to try to reduce global warming before it is too late.

NATURAL HAZARDS

DREADFUL DROUGHTS

Rain may ruin your summer holidays or force you to cancel a barbecue, but life would be very difficult without it. All living things need water – there isn't a plant, animal or human being on the planet that can survive for too long without it. If seasonal rains fail to arrive, this can cause serious problems for people and animals.

What Causes Droughts?

A drought occurs when the climate is hotter and drier than it normally would be – sometimes for several months, or even years. Droughts can strike almost anywhere, but they are more likely and more severe in areas where rainfall is unreliable, such as the Great Plains of the USA, the Sahel area of Africa and central Australia.

There are several different reasons for weather to change enough to cause a drought – here are a few of them:

Global Warming. Most scientists agree that the world is getting warmer due to the enhanced greenhouse effect (see pages 27 to 28). Higher temperatures mean less rain falls and more water evaporates from the soil, leaving it dry. Scientists predict that global warming means droughts will get worse in areas where they are already common. They may also start to affect places where rain is usually plentiful.

El Niño. This is a weather system that can cause serious flooding as well as droughts. It happens every three to seven years.

Scientists believe that El Niño is caused by the surface of the eastern Pacific Ocean warming up. The normal pattern of weather over the southern Pacific is then reversed – rains fail to fall in parts of Australia and Southeast Asia. This causes terrible droughts when these areas should be in their rainy season.

El Niño also brings rain, violent storms and flooding to parts of South America, such as Peru and Ecuador.

Pressure Changes. Rain clouds are formed in bands of low-pressure air called 'depressions'. If a band of rain meets an area of high pressure (see page 20), the high pressure prevents the moist air from rising. This means that clouds do not form, so there's no rain. If the high pressure prevents rain falling for some time, there will be a drought.

This can happen even in relatively cool areas of the planet, such as the British Isles.

I JUST WANNA WALLOW.

The Inter-Tropical Convergence Zone (ITCZ). This is a band of clouds around the equator where warm trade winds blowing from the northern and southern hemispheres meet, or 'converge'. When they meet, they rise high in the sky, causing the air and moisture to cool quickly. This cooling air then forms huge rain clouds. The position of the ITCZ varies with the seasons, as it moves north and south following the position of the Sun (see page 19).

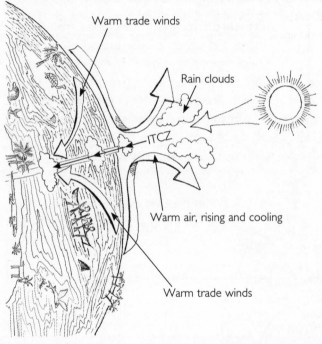

Warm trade winds

Rain clouds

ITCZ

Warm air, rising and cooling

Warm trade winds

The movement of the ITCZ and its rain clouds means that over the course of a year, places in the tropics have wet and dry seasons. In some years, the ITCZ doesn't move as far north or south as usual, and tropical continents, such as Africa, don't get enough rain. If this happens for several years, it causes a drought, which can be devastating.

What Happens Next?

When drought hits, a number of things can happen:

Water Shortages. Lack of rain and water-loss by evaporation means river levels drop, and stores of water in the soil and under the ground fall. People may have to walk huge distances to find water to drink and wash in.

Food Shortages And Famine. Plants can't grow properly without water, so over time, farmers' crops fail and vegetation dies. Terrible food shortage, when people and animals die from starvation, is known as 'famine'.

Diseases. In poorer countries, when regular water supplies dry up, people may be forced to drink dirty water. This can cause deadly diseases, such as cholera. Sometimes, people have no choice but to leave their homes and go to refugee camps in search of food, water and medical care.

Drought-Busters

Incredibly, there are many plants and animals that are 'drought-proof' and are able to survive for long periods without rainfall. These include:

Cactuses. These spiky desert-dwellers are examples of plants known as 'xerophytes' (pronounced 'zeh-roh-fites'), which means that they are adapted to hot, dry climates. They have large, shallow roots that spread over a wide area to maximize the amount of water they can take from the ground. They can also store water in their stems.

Baobab Trees. The bizarre-looking baobab tree grows in Africa, Australia and Madagascar. The tree is extremely tough and has an enormous trunk, which can store thousands of gallons of water during the dry season. Its rubbery trunk can even survive burning!

Camels. These creatures are called the 'ships of the desert', as they are used to travel across dry regions, often carrying heavy loads. Their thick coats reflect sunlight and keep them cool. Long eyelashes help to keep sand out of their eyes, and they can even shut their nostrils to keep out sand. Many people think a camel's hump is full of water, but in fact it contains fat. This acts as a food store, allowing them to travel for many days without food.

Lungfish. Unlike other fish, which breathe through gills to take oxygen from water, lungfish have lungs. They come to the surface to breathe air – just as their name suggests! These clever fish can survive months or even years of drought by burrowing into the mud at the bottom of a river before the water dries up. They surround themselves with a sticky substance called mucus, that hardens and protects them until the dry season is over.

WILDFIRES

A wildfire is an outdoor fire that gets out of control and runs, well … wild. They can be destructive forces of nature and their unpredictability makes them extremely dangerous.

Whipping Up A Wildfire

For any fire to start, it needs three things: fuel, heat and oxygen. This is sometimes known as the 'fire triangle'. When firefighters are battling a blazing fire, they try to break the triangle by removing one of the three things feeding it, so it can be put out.

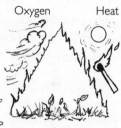

Oxygen   Heat

Fuel

In the case of wildfires, dry wood, grass and plants are the fuel, the oxygen comes from the air, and the heat needed can come from the tiniest of sparks – a lightning strike, a campfire or even the heat from the Sun on a very hot day.

Once a wildfire has started, it spreads very quickly. The flames and smoke heat up the fuel in the surrounding area, drying it out, and setting it on fire as well. The largest wildfires recorded have happened on dry, windy days with low humidity (meaning that the air has very little moisture in it).

The wind fans the flames of the fire, providing it with more oxygen and blowing sparks and embers of fire on to vegetation that is further away. The natural whirling and swirling of wind makes tracking and containing wildfires extremely difficult, as they can change direction as suddenly as the wind can.

Feeling The Heat

A raging wildfire can sweep through an area with speeds of up to 23km/h. It burns with an intense heat, destroying almost everything in its path.

It's not just the heat that makes wildfires so deadly. The flames can be many metres high, the smoke will make it difficult to breathe, and the sound of tinder-dry wood crackling and flames raging will be almost deafening. Here are some of the effects of a large-scale wildfire:

Toxic Gas Pollution. Large amounts of smoke are generated by these out-of-control blazes. This smoke contains tiny particles that can cause breathing problems if inhaled. In 1997, Indonesia had many wildfires, which were started as people tried to clear land for farming. They burned out of control for many months. They produced smoke that blanketed six countries across Southeast Asia, affecting more than 70 million people. It is likely the health of people who breathed in these particles may be affected in years to come, as they can cause damage to the lungs, kidneys, liver and nervous system.

Wildlife Deaths. Many animals are lost every year due to wildfires. The terrible fires that struck Australia in 2009 are believed to have killed millions of animals, including kangaroos, koalas, lizards and birds. Many kangaroos that were lucky enough to escape the flames were scorched when they tried to return to their homes, as the smouldering ground singed their feet.

Loss Of Life And Property. Fortunately, humans are getting better at tackling and predicting natural hazards, but fires can move fast and change direction unexpectedly, leaving people trapped. During a wildfire, many people have to leave their homes to burn, sacrificing everything they have to the hungry flames.

Damage To Soil. After a wildfire, destroyed vegetation leaves the soil bare, so it is unprotected from storms and rain. Soil can easily be washed away, taking valuable nutrients with it, and causing floods and landslides. This is called soil erosion. Scientists have found that this can be reduced by covering the bare ground with straw, and by replanting with grasses as soon as possible.

Burning Benefits?

It would be easy to think that all wildfires are bad, but in some environments, fires are a necessary process that allow nature to flourish rather than die.

Man-made fires in forests and on grassland have been used for many hundreds of years. This method is called controlled or prescribed burning, and should only be attempted by fire-trained professionals who know how to keep the flames from getting out of hand. Here are a few of the fiery benefits:

• Farmers in Africa's savannah grasslands deliberately burn fields of vegetation to get rid of the crop stubble and return nutrients to the soil. This helps to keep the land fertile for the next crop.

• Controlled fires in forests clear areas of unwanted vegetation, so the trees and plants do not have to compete with each other for sunlight and nutrients.

• Setting a controlled blaze in the canopy, or top leafy layer, of trees allows the sunlight to penetrate through to the forest floor.

• Some plant species actually need fire to aid their seed germination. For example, the Banksia plant, from Australia, keeps its seeds tightly locked away in capsules until scorched open by fire.

World's Worst Wildfires

• One of Australia's worst days of fires was 7th February 2009, following a severe heatwave in the state of Victoria. The fires claimed the lives of 173 people and destroyed thousands of homes. This day has become known in Australia as Black Saturday.

• In June and July of 1998, wildfires in Florida, USA, forced more than 35,000 people out of their homes. They needed over 5,000 firefighters to put out blazes.

• In July 2010, huge forest fires raced through parts of central Russia, destroying whole villages and leaving thousands homeless. The fires started thanks to Russia's worst drought for more than a century.

• In North America, there are around 50,000 wildfires every year. Four out of five of them are started by people's carelessness. Discarded cigarettes and campfires that haven't been put out are the most common causes.

• Throughout the summer of 2007, Greece was plagued by enormous forest fires, which killed 84 people. Important historical sites, such as the city of Athens and Olympia, the birthplace of the Olympics, were threatened by the flames.

NASTY ERUPTIONS

A volcano is the point at which 'magma', or liquid rock, from the Earth's mantle, erupts through the ground (see pages 10 to 11). Pressure forces either magma or hot, volcanic ash out of the ground through a 'vent', or hole, in the Earth's surface, making spectacular, but dangerous, displays.

Molten Mountains

Volcanoes can form anywhere on Earth, from ocean floors to beneath glaciers. However, they usually form along the edges of tectonic plates, where the different sections of the planet's surface push towards or pull away from each other (see pages 12 to 15). Magma builds up in huge underground chambers and erupts as 'lava', the name for magma once it is above ground. At temperatures of between 700°C and 1,250°C, lava is dangerously hot and destructive. It can be thick and slow-moving like jam, runny like a thin custard, or anything in between. As it cools, the lava hardens, forming new rock, including pumice (pronounced 'puh-miss'). Over time, different volcano shapes build up depending on the 'viscosity', or

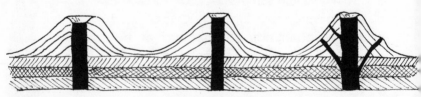

Dome Volcanoes
The lava from these volcanoes is acidic and solidifies very quickly, making a rounded dome with steep sides.

Ash And Cinder Volcanoes
These volcanoes are created by ash instead of lava and their shape depends on how steeply the ash can settle. They tend to have curved sides that become more gentle towards the bottom.

Composite Volcanoes
These are large and old volcanoes made up of layers of both ash and lava from different types of explosions.

thickness, of the lava. The thickness varies according to the type of rock that is melted and how much pressure is inside the volcano. The different types of volcano, categorized according to the shape, are described in the diagram below.

Hot Spots!

'Hot spots' are super-heated areas below the Earth's crust. These cause the crust to melt, allowing magma to escape and build volcanoes – even away from plate margins. Hot spots can keep volcanoes erupting for centuries, but as the Earth's tectonic plate shifts, the land moves away from the hot spot and its magma so the volcano becomes 'dormant', or resting, and cannot erupt (see pages 69 to 70).

Volcanic Benefits

Some volcanic places, such as Iceland and New Zealand, have 'geysers', or hot springs. These produce hot water and jets of steam which can be used to heat homes and provide electricity. They are also popular tourist destinations. Volcanic eruptions also produce mineral-rich rock, creating some of the world's most fertile farm land.

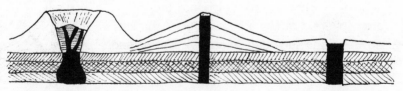

Crater Volcanoes
(also known as calderas)
These form during very violent eruptions, normally after a large build-up of gas beneath the volcano. Often these volcanoes have large blown-out craters caused by explosive eruptions.

Shield Volcanoes
Very runny lava means these volcanoes have quite gentle slopes. However, continuous build-up of lava layers from repeated eruptions means they can be very wide.

Fissure Volcanoes
Found at constructive ocean plates (see page 15), these sometimes look like cracks along the Earth's surface and have very gentle slopes. The lava is runny and can flow over large distances.

Don't Fall In!

A series of volcanoes known as the Circum-Pacific Belt, or Ring of Fire, arcs around the Pacific Ocean in a horseshoe shape. This area is teeming with hot spots and 'seismic' activity (which is the plate movement that causes volcanic eruptions and earthquakes). It is where most of the planet's 'active', or regularly erupting, volcanoes lie.

How To 'Lava' Volcano

There are many different types of eruption and they can have some pretty scary results:

Pyroclastic Flow. This occurs after an explosive eruption, sending an avalanche of rock, gases, pumice and ash flowing down the volcano at speeds of more than 100km/h, and temperatures of more than 500°C, burning everything in its path.

Plinian Eruption. When these happen, gas and rock is sent shooting high into the atmosphere, forming a huge cloud. Ash rains down on the surrounding area. This is named after Pliny the Younger, a Roman who carefully recorded the eruption of Mount Vesuvius in CE 79, which destroyed the city of Pompeii.

Phreatic Eruption. These eruptions happen when magma erupts into water at the surface, instantly boiling it. In a phreatic (pronounced 'fray-attic') eruption, steam, ash and large rocks, or 'bombs', can shoot out from the volcano.

Volcanic Attack!

Lava flows can destroy pretty much anything in their path, but there's even more to the dangers of volcanoes. Here are just a few of them:

Lahars. These are volcanic mudflows of ash and debris, which mix with water to form deadly mudslides. The water can be a result of heavy rain just after an eruption, or when eruptions melt ice on a snow-capped volcano. On steep slopes, a lahar can travel at speeds that are more than fast enough to knock down trees and bury houses.

Dust Clouds. Volcanoes can spread dust clouds across the globe, blocking out the Sun and lowering the temperature. If the layers of ash are very thick, the temperature can be lowered for years. In 1815, Mount Tambora erupted, sending so much dust into the atmosphere that 1816 was known as 'the year without a summer'.

Flooding. Volcanic eruptions can also cause flooding – especially when they occur underwater. They can create giant waves called tsunamis (see page 107). In 1883, the eruption of Krakatau, in Indonesia, created a wave that was 40 metres high. It is estimated that more than 36,000 people were killed.

Did You Know?

The word 'volcano' is taken from the name Vulcan, the god of fire in Roman mythology. It was believed he made weapons for the gods in the fires of Vulcano, an island off the coast of Sicily.

ENORMOUS EARTHQUAKES

Earthquakes usually take place along fault planes – where tectonic plates meet (see pages 12 to 15). The shaking or rolling below the planet's surface when two plates slip past each other can be slight enough that you can hardly feel it, or so violent that whole cities are destroyed.

Whose Fault Is It?

More than 80 % of all earthquakes happen in the Ring of Fire (see page 102), making it the shakiest place on the planet, but earthquakes can happen wherever plate boundaries come together.

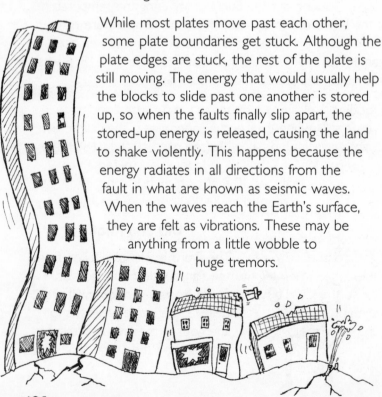

While most plates move past each other, some plate boundaries get stuck. Although the plate edges are stuck, the rest of the plate is still moving. The energy that would usually help the blocks to slide past one another is stored up, so when the faults finally slip apart, the stored-up energy is released, causing the land to shake violently. This happens because the energy radiates in all directions from the fault in what are known as seismic waves. When the waves reach the Earth's surface, they are felt as vibrations. These may be anything from a little wobble to huge tremors.

How Shocking

Some earthquakes begin with little tremors, or 'foreshocks', that happen in advance of the main shock. The main shock is the largest and most violent part and is followed by smaller earthquakes called 'aftershocks'. If the main shock is really big, the aftershocks can go on for days, months or even years.

Although many plate boundaries are under the oceans, there are some on land. The best-known is the San Andreas fault, which stretches for more than 900 kilometres along the west coast of the United States, passing through two large cities, San Francisco and Los Angeles. There are frequent earthquakes along the fault.

Breaking Waves

Seismic waves can travel thousands of kilometres around the Earth and cause a lot of damage. So how do these waves shake things up so much?

Primary (P) waves are the first waves you feel. They travel at super-speeds, stretching and compressing the Earth. They can move at speeds of up to 6km/sec. Secondary (S) waves, are half as fast as P waves, but they really shake things up as they ripple through the ground.

Once P waves and S waves have moved through the ground, surface waves arrive. They might be the last to get there, but when they do, they don't go unnoticed. They cause the Earth's surface to shake up and down, making the ground roll and ripple, in a similar way to waves on the surface of the ocean. Some earthquake scientists, or seismologists, describe the slow surface waves as the sting in an earthquake's tail.

How To Measure An Earthquake

Seismologists record and monitor the 'magnitude', or strength, of earthquakes using instruments called seismographs to measure the waves. They can use the time that the waves arrive at different monitoring stations and their strength when they get there to work out where and when the earthquake has taken place.

There are a number of ways to describe the strength of an earthquake. The best-known was developed by an American man named Charles Richter in the 1930s. Each number on the Richter scale (pronounced 'rick-ter') describes an earthquake ten times greater than the number before. This means that an earthquake measuring 2.0 on the Richter scale is ten times stronger than one measuring 1.0, and an earthquake measuring 3.0 is one hundred times greater than one of 1.0, and so on.

The largest earthquake ever measured on the Richter scale was in Chile, South America, in 1960. It had a magnitude of 9.5, and left more than two million people homeless.

Earthquakes can also be described on a scale from 'minor' – 3.9 or less – to 'great' – more than 8.0. Scientists estimate that there can be as many as 900,000 very minor 'micro-earthquakes', of 2.5 or less, a year. These are so small that you usually can't feel them, but they can be recorded by seismographs. A great earthquake can destroy a whole town if it is located at the 'epicentre', which is the point at which the earthquake originates. However, earthquakes of this size usually only happen every five to ten years.

Earth-Shattering Effects

Major earthquakes can be very deadly and result in buildings collapsing, and roads and bridges being destroyed. The shaking can make the ground become like jelly, damaging electricity and gas cabling, which causes fires. Landslides and avalanches can also be triggered by earthquakes and, if the epicentre is located in the ocean, an earthquake can create a huge wave, called a 'tsunami'.

A tsunami is triggered when water in the ocean is moved violently. This sets off a ripple effect, and the waves travel across the oceans. In open water, they travel fast and a great distance apart, but as they reach shallower water, they slow down and pile up to form a wall of water up to 40 metres high. Often, the lowest point of the wave, called the trough, hits the beach first, resulting in 'drawback', when the water is sucked back out to sea before the wall of water strikes. This can be the only warning that a tsunami is approaching.

In December 2004, a huge tsunami struck in Indonesia, Southeast Asia, after an earthquake in the Indian Ocean measuring more than 9.0 on the Richter scale. It struck across a huge part of the globe, including Thailand, Sri Lanka, the Indonesian province of Banda Aceh and the coast of Somalia, in Africa. More than 200,000 people were killed, and more than 1.5 million people were left homeless.

CYCLONES

Tropical cyclones are huge, circular storms of heavy rain, cloud and winds that form over warm, tropical waters. Depending on where they happen, these storms can also be known as hurricanes or typhoons.

How To Make A Hurricane

Cyclones, typhoons and hurricanes mainly happen between July and September in the northern hemisphere, and January and March in the southern hemisphere. These storms develop over oceans where the temperature is at least 27 °C and the water is around 60 metres deep. The storm must start at least 500 kilometres from the equator so that the Earth's rotation will help it to spin. Warm air circulates above the water, rising and evaporating in the cooler air above. An area of very low pressure is created (see page 20), which then makes the winds move more quickly.

These storms bring torrential rains, strong winds and huge waves, called a 'storm surge', that cause a lot of damage when they come ashore. Tropical cyclones have also been known to cause landslides and mudslides, and, of course, the storm surges and heavy rain can cause serious flooding.

The Eye Of The Storm

A hurricane can be more than 1,000 kilometres wide with winds of more than 160km/h. The area at the centre, however, known as the 'eye of the storm', can be so calm that there is almost no breeze at all. The eye is usually 30 kilometres to 60 kilometres wide and, once it passes, the most dangerous part of the storm arrives – the eyewall.

Here the rain is stronger than elsewhere in the storm and it may contain raging thunderstorms.

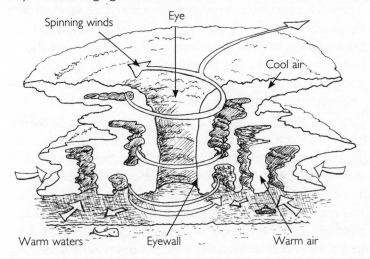

Spinning winds • Eye • Cool air • Warm waters • Eyewall • Warm air

Tropical Travellers

The paths that cyclones take are very unpredictable, though they generally move in a westward direction. It can take up to two weeks for a cyclone to blow itself out, causing mayhem wherever it goes.

The Name Game

You may have heard cyclones called by names such as 'Fran' and 'John', but how does a tropical storm get its name?

Meteorologists have an alphabetical list of names to use each year, with a different list for different regions. When a storm is strong enough to be classified as a cyclone, it is given the next free name on the list. If a storm is particularly violent and causes a great deal of damage and loss of life, the name is retired and not used again.

TWISTING TORNADOES

Tornadoes occur during severe thunderstorms when strong winds transform into a twisting column of air, turning at speeds of up to 500km/h. They last just minutes, but the winds of a tornado are so powerful they have even been known to lift objects the size of cars and drive blades of straw into the trunks of trees.

Funnel Formation

Tornadoes form when cool, dry air from the north meets warm, moist air from the south, creating a thunderstorm. Air starts to circulate when warm air at ground level rises, and cool air in the troposphere (see page 17) above sinks, rotating along the ground. Rising air lifts the spinning winds into a vertical column called a 'funnel cloud'. This sucks air up at speeds of as much as 300km/h, and the spinning air stretches towards the ground in a pipe, becoming a tornado. This can remain relatively still, or travel at speeds between 40km/h and 90km/h. If it reaches ground level, it can cause chaos.

Tornado Touchdown

Most reported tornadoes happen in the USA, where there are around 1,000 per year. The majority of them take place in what is known as 'Tornado Alley'. This central area goes through the states of Nebraska, Kansas, Oklahoma and Texas. Texas alone has an average of 125 tornadoes a year!

Did You Know?

The majority of tornadoes in the northern hemisphere rotate anticlockwise – the majority of tornadoes in the southern hemisphere rotate clockwise.

Spring And Summer Spinners

Tornadoes can happen at any time of year, but the spring and summer months see more tornadoes than at other times of year.

What's more, you are more likely to see a tornado between 3pm and 7pm local time than at other times of day as there has been time for the ground to heat up, creating perfect 'twister' conditions. However, most tornadoes are only at ground level for about ten minutes, and only 2% of all tornadoes recorded are extremely damaging.

111

What's The Damage?

Scientists estimate the speeds of tornadoes' winds in 3-second gusts and give them an 'EF' number – short for the Enhanced Fujita scale. This number is based on the damage done to any buildings and trees as a tornado passes by:

EF-Number	3-Second Gust
0	105–137km/h (65–85 mph)
1	138–177km/h (86–110 mph)
2	178–217km/h (111–135 mph)
3	218–265km/h (136–165 mph)
4	266–322km/h (166–200 mph)
5	322+km/h (200+ mph)

The damage caused can range from broken tree branches (EF 0) to total destruction (EF 5).

It's A Twister

Tornadoes can cause real damage. If a terrifying tornado ever whips through your area, you'll want to be prepared. Currently, the average warning time for a tornado alert is about 11 minutes. Warning signs include a dark, greenish sky, large hailstorms, and a powerful train-like roar. If a tornado is on the way – take shelter quickly!

Did You Know?

The fastest wind speed ever measured is 511km/h, which was recorded during a tornado near Oklahoma City, USA, in 1999.

INCREDIBLE COUNTRIES AND AMAZING MAPS

COUNTRIES AND CONTINENTS

Most geographers divide the planet's land masses into seven continents, based on a combination of their geographic features and the underlying plate tectonics (see page 12). Asia is the largest continent, followed by Africa, North America, South America, Antarctica, Europe and Oceania.

Each continent is divided into different countries. Political events mean that people sometimes decide to join two countries together or to make a region into a new independent country. This means that the total number of countries in the world can change.

On the following pages are lists of all the countries in each continent, along with their capital cities. The countries of Central America, which sits between North and South America, and the Caribbean have been listed separately to make them easier to locate on a map. However, officially they belong with North America.

Asia

Asia is the world's largest continent covering 44,614,000km². It covers almost 30% of the world's land area and contains 60% of the world's population. It is the only continent that borders two other continents – Africa and Europe. It sometimes also joins with a third continent, North America, in the winter when ice forms in the Bering Sea.

Country	Capital	Country	Capital
Afghanistan	Kabul	Bhutan	Thimphu
Armenia	Yerevan	Brunei	Bandar Seri
Azerbaijan	Baku		Begawan
Bahrain	Manama	Cambodia	Phnom Penh
Bangladesh	Dhaka	China	Beijing

Country	Capital	Country	Capital
East Timor (officially Democratic Republic of Timor-Leste)	Dili	Nepal	Kathmandu
		North Korea	Pyongyang
		Oman	Muscat
Georgia	Tbilisi	Pakistan	Islamabad
India	New Delhi	Philippines	Manila
Indonesia	Jakarta	Qatar	Doha
Iran	Tehran	Russia (Russian Federation)	Moscow (also Europe)
Iraq	Baghdad	Saudi Arabia	Riyadh
Israel	Jerusalem	Singapore	Singapore
Japan	Tokyo	South Korea	Seoul
Jordan	Amman	Sri Lanka	Colombo † Sri Jayawar-denepura ††
Kazakhstan	Astana		
Korea, see North Korea and South Korea		Syria	Damascus
		Taiwan	Taipei
Kuwait	Kuwait City	Tajikistan	Dushanbe
Kyrgyzstan	Bishkek	Thailand	Bangkok
Laos	Vientiane	Turkey	Ankara (also Europe)
Lebanon	Beirut		
Malaysia	Kuala Lumpur	Turkmenistan	Ashgabat
Maldives	Male	United Arab Emirates	Abu Dhabi
Mongolia	Ulaanbaatar		
Myanmar (formerly Burma)	Nay Pyi Taw	Uzbekistan	Tashkent
		Vietnam	Hanoi
		Yemen	Sanaa

† Executive capital, where the laws are carried out
†† Legislative and judicial capital, where laws are made, the country's judges sit and trials are held

Africa

This is the world's second largest continent. Africa covers an area of 30,348,110km². It is estimated that more than 2,000 languages are spoken across the continent.

Country	Capital
Algeria	Algiers
Angola	Luanda
Benin	Porto-Novo
Botswana	Gaborone
Burkina Faso	Ouagadougou
Burundi	Bujumbura
Cameroon	Yaoundé
Cape Verde	Praia
Central African Republic	Bangui
Chad	N'Djamena
Comoros	Moroni
Congo (officially Republic of the Congo)	Brazzaville
Congo (Democratic Republic of the Congo)	Kinshasa
Côte D'Ivoire (formerly Ivory Coast)	Yamoussoukro * Abidjan **
Djibouti	Djibouti
Egypt	Cairo
Equatorial Guinea	Malabo
Eritrea	Asmara
Ethiopia	Addis Ababa
Gabon	Libreville
Gambia, The	Banjul
Ghana	Accra
Guinea	Conakry
Guinea-Bissau	Bissau
Kenya	Nairobi
Lesotho	Maseru
Liberia	Monrovia
Libya	Tripoli
Madagascar	Antananarivo
Malawi	Lilongwe
Mali	Bamako
Mauritania	Nouakchott
Mauritius	Port Louis
Morocco	Rabat
Mozambique	Maputo
Namibia	Windhoek
Niger	Niamey
Nigeria	Abuja
Rwanda	Kigali
São Tomé and Príncipe	São Tomé
Senegal	Dakar
Seychelles	Victoria
Sierra Leone	Freetown
Somalia	Mogadishu
South Africa	Pretoria † Bloemfontein †† Cape Town †††

* Official capital
** 'De facto' capital, meaning the unofficial centre of government

† Executive capital, where the laws are carried out
†† Judicial capital, where the country's judges sit and trials are held
††† Legislative capital, where laws are made

Country	Capital	Country	Capital
Sudan	*Khartoum*	Tunisia	*Tunis*
South Sudan	*Juba*	Uganda	*Kampala*
Swaziland	*Mbabane*	Zambia	*Lusaka*
Tanzania	*Dodoma ‡*	Zimbabwe	*Harare*
	Dar es Salaam ‡‡		
Togo	*Lomé*		

North America

North America is the third largest continent on Earth with a total area of 24,247,039km². The largest city in North America is Mexico City, the capital of Mexico, but the largest country in North America in terms of population is the USA (United States of America).

Country	Capital	Country	Capital
Canada	*Ottawa*	United States	
Mexico	*Mexico City*	of America	*Washington D.C.*

‡ Official capital   ‡‡ Former capital, where parts of the government are still located

Central America And The Caribbean

An important feature of Central America is the Panama Canal, which took ten years to build and opened in 1914. The canal allows ships to cross Central America from the Pacific Ocean to the Atlantic Ocean. It cuts 50 miles across the country of Panama and saves ships from having to sail thousands of miles around South America.

Country	Capital	Country	Capital
Antigua		Haiti	Port-au-Prince
and Barbuda	St John's	Honduras	Tegucigalpa
Bahamas, The	Nassau	Jamaica	Kingston
Barbados	Bridgetown	Nicaragua	Managua
Belize	Belmopan	Panama	Panama City
Costa Rica	San José	Saint Kitts	
Cuba	Havana	and Nevis	Basseterre
Dominica	Roseau	Saint Lucia	Castries
Dominican		Saint Vincent and	
Republic	Santo Domingo	the Grenadines	Kingstown
El Salvador	San Salvador	Trinidad	
Grenada	Saint George's	and Tobago	Port of Spain
Guatemala	Guatemala City		

South America

South America covers 17,827,340km² and stretches from the hot and humid tropics to the chilly South Atlantic. The largest South American country, in both size and population, is Brazil. The continent is also home to the world's highest waterfall, Salto Ángel, or Angel Falls, which is 979 metres tall!

Country	Capital	Country	Capital
Argentina	*Buenos Aires*	Ecuador	*Quito*
Bolivia	*La Paz †*	Guyana	*Georgetown*
	Sucre ††	Paraguay	*Asunción*
Brazil	*Brasilia*	Peru	*Lima*
Chile	*Santiago*	Suriname	*Paramaribo*
Colombia	*Bogotá*	Uruguay	*Montevideo*
		Venezuela	*Caracas*

Europe

Europe is the second smallest continent on Earth, covering 10,400,000km². It is home to many of the world's oldest countries including the five oldest: San Marino, France, Bulgaria, Denmark and Portugal.

It also boasts the smallest country in the world, Vatican City, which is the smallest country both in size and population.

Country	Capital	Country	Capital
Albania	*Tirana*	Bulgaria	*Sofia*
Andorra	*Andorra la Vella*	Croatia	*Zagreb*
Austria	*Vienna*	Cyprus	*Nicosia*
Belarus	*Minsk*	Czech Republic	*Prague*
Belgium	*Brussels*	Denmark	*Copenhagen*
Bosnia and		Estonia	*Tallinn*
Herzegovina	*Sarajevo*	Finland	*Helsinki*

† Administrative capital, where the main government is run
†† Judicial capital, where the country's judges sit and trials are held

Country	Capital	Country	Capital
France	Paris	Norway	Oslo
Germany	Berlin	Poland	Warsaw
Greece	Athens	Portugal	Lisbon
Hungary	Budapest	Romania	Bucharest
Iceland	Reykjavik	Russia (Russian	Moscow
Ireland	Dublin	Federation)	(also Asia)
Italy	Rome	San Marino	San Marino
Kosovo	Pristina	Serbia	Belgrade
(declared itself independent, 2008)		Slovakia	Bratislava
Latvia	Riga	Slovenia	Ljubljana
Liechtenstein	Vaduz	Spain	Madrid
Lithuania	Vilnius	Sweden	Stockholm
Luxembourg	Luxembourg	Switzerland	Bern
Macedonia	Skopje	Turkey	Ankara
Malta	Valletta		
Moldova	Chişinău	(also Asia)	
Monaco	Monaco	Ukraine	Kiev
Montenegro	Podgorica	United Kingdom	London
Netherlands	Amsterdam *	Vatican City	Vatican City
	The Hague **		

* Official capital, where the laws are carried out
** The city from which the country is governed

Oceania/Australia

Oceania covers a land area of 8,508,238km². There are more sheep in Oceania than people. The largest country in Oceania is Australia, which is sometimes considered a continent by itself.

Oceania is located in the southern hemisphere. This means that winter is during June, July and August, and summer during the months of December, January, and February.

Country	Capital	Country	Capital
Australia	Canberra	Palau	Melekeok
Fiji	Suva	Papua	
Kiribati	Bairiki	New Guinea	Port Moresby
Marshall Islands	Majuro	Samoa	Apia
Micronesia		Solomon Islands	Honiara
(Federated States		Tonga	Nuku'alofa
of Micronesia)	Palikir	Tuvalu	Funafuti
Nauru	Yaren	Vanuatu	Port Vila
New Zealand	Wellington		

Antarctica

Antarctica is a little unusual, because it doesn't 'belong' to a single country. It covers an area of around 14,200,000km², and it is believed to be rich in minerals. Various countries have tried to lay claim to the land, but it is now governed by international treaty to protect it. The only people who brave the inhospitable land are a few thousand scientists.

THE MARVEL OF MAPS

Maps can look dull and rather baffling at first glance. However, a family outing without a map might end in argument; a walk in the country might have you going around in circles – and what use would a pirate be without knowing where to hunt for the buried treasure?

Being able to understand maps is a very useful skill and, even if you aren't a pirate, one that could possibly save your life one day.

Map Basics

Maps show you a bird's-eye view of places. There are many different types, from street maps, to satellite images, to Ordnance Survey (OS) maps and atlases. Each type of map tells you something different about a place. To start to read a map, you need to know which way up it goes. On a map, north is always at the top and the simplest way to find north is with a compass.

The four main points of a compass are north, east, south and west. Remember them more easily with this saying:

Never **E**at **S**hredded **W**heat.

The initial letter of each word reminds you of the order of the compass directions from the top and going clockwise around the compass.

The four main points in between each of the main compass points are northeast, southeast, southwest and northwest.

Once you have the compass needle lined up with north, you can turn the top of your map to face the same way.

How Far Is It?

If you want to get from A to B safely, you need to know how far away your destination is and how long it will take to get there. You can work this out by looking at what is called the 'scale' of the map – how many centimetres on the map is equal to one metre or kilometre in real life. Your map should have a scale line that you can measure distances against.

Measuring straight-line distances is easy. Just place the straight edge of a piece of paper between the two points you are measuring. Mark the two points on the paper, then place it along the scale line to work out the true distance.

Measuring lines that are not so straight can be done using a piece of string to follow the map, again marking it with your pen and reading it against the scale line.

Once you know how far away your destination is, you'll be able to work out roughly how long it will take you to arrive.

Grid Lines

Grid lines run horizontally and vertically on maps. Each one has a number that can help you to find places more quickly. To do this, you need to have what is called a 'grid reference', which is a six figure number – 123456, for example. The first three numbers (123) refer to the boxes running along the map from left to right. The last three numbers (456) refer to the boxes running up the map.

The first number from the first group (1) tells you how far along the map to look. The first number from the second group (4) tells you how far up the map to look. The rest of the numbers give you more exact locations in each direction. Remember this saying:

> Along the corridor and up the stairs.

This reminds you that the first set of numbers refers to the boxes going along the map from left to right, and that the second set refers to the boxes going up the map.

Symbols

Maps are full of information to help you, but with so much going on, map-makers need to use symbols to cram everything in and to make things really clear.

Each map has what is called a 'key' to help you. This is a list of all the symbols that appear on the map with the meaning written alongside. There are symbols for different types of road, railway lines, forests and parks, rivers and lakes and much, much more.

Maps – you'd be lost without them!